present
tense

present tense

a
Mennonite
spirituality

Gordon Houser

Foreword by
Richard Rohr

Cascadia
Publishing House
Telford, Pennsylvania

Cascadia Publishing House orders, information, reprint permissions:
contact@CascadiaPublishingHouse.com
1-215-723-9125
126 Klingerman Road, Telford PA 18969
www.CascadiaPublishingHouse.com

Present Tense
Copyright © 2011 by Cascadia Publishing House.
Telford, PA 18969
All rights reserved
DreamSeeker Books is an imprint of Cascadia Publishing House LLC
Library of Congress Catalog Number: 2011028334
ISBN 13: 978-1-931038-90-4; ISBN 10: 1-931038-90-2
Book design by Cascadia Publishing House
Cover design by Dawn Ranck

Library of Congress Cataloguing-in-Publication Data
Houser, Gordon.
Present tense : a Mennonite spirituality / by Gordon Houser.
    p. cm.
Summary: "Gordon Houser explores the heart of Mennonite spirituality and
how Mennonite spiritual practices may succeed or fall short."--Provided by pub-
lisher.
Includes bibliographical references (p.   ).
ISBN-13: 978-1-931038-90-4 (alk. paper)
ISBN-10: 1-931038-90-2 (alk. paper)
1. Christian life--Mennonite authors. 2. Spirituality--Mennonites. 3. Houser,
Gordon. I. Title.

BV4501.3.H6817 2011
248.4'897--dc23

2011028334

17 16 15 14 13 12 11   10 9 8 7 6 5 4 3 2 1

For Jeanne,
my companion and teacher

Contents

Foreword

After having so many Mennonite friends and acquaintances over the years, I have often said that if I had not been born Catholic and had to choose my Christian denomination, I would without a doubt choose to be a Mennonite! That is still true, and that despite my beginnings, just like Gordon Houser—in lovely "over the rainbow" Kansas!

We Catholic Kansans, ghettoized in a Protestant Republican state in the 1950s, could never understand why those Mennonites always voted Republican (at least in those days!). This always seemed to us like the political party of money, power, and war, which was exactly what Mennonites neither believed in nor lived. This group just did not make much sense.

Mennonites were a living example of Thomas Frank's thesis in *What's the Matter with Kansas*, that Kansas people are the textbook example of people who consistently vote against their own legitimate self interest—and don't even know it. I could only conclude that they must be another confused Protestant sect. Yet Menno Simons, I heard, was a rather enlightened Catholic priest. So I remained the confused one myself for many years, and it took real Mennonites to un-confuse me. Or should I better say, re-confuse me?

At any rate, I finally got the historical explanation for their politics and eventually met real Mennonites in Cincinnati, Normal, Illinois, South Bend, Indiana, on the road, and here in Albuquerque, and all of my remaining prejudices and confusions vanished. Though they too must have their shadows, I myself have yet to meet a Mennonite I did not like or admire. Really. Why is it that one group can get so much of the gospel so right—and without a fully centralized authority mandating uniform belief or even requiring a fundamentalist or rigid reading of the Scriptures? And be nice besides! For a Catholic this was a major discovery and allurement. It told me that there must be another way to convene and deepen a Christian people, and whatever it was, the Mennonites seemed to have found it.

Well, I wonder if this book might not give you some strong clues as to precisely what Mennonites have found. I remember when Gordon as a young man used to write to me when I was a young priest in faraway Cincinnati. He was already on a good spiritual search then. I'm not sure how he discovered me, but he would seek my long-distance advice. You need to know that this was rather rare in the still-divided denominations of the 1970s. His humility humbled me.

Somehow the Mennonites seem to have found an inspired balancing act between practice, lifestyle, community, and Scripture. Their lovely "Franciscan" humility also keeps them strongly teachable and open. They seem to revel in self-deprecating humor, which is not so common among Christians. To use present categories, Mennonites seem to have found a fine integration of the best of very conservative gospel values with the best of progressive and critical thinking, especially in regard to the prophetic thrust of the gospel—yet without becoming righteous or dogmatic. How rare that is!

As a Franciscan, I would say about Mennonites what I have always said about St. Francis himself. He was a "fundamentalist" of sorts, but he was fundamentalist about the right things. Not demanding or judgmental of others but always demanding more of himself. Not emphasizing or arguing about doctrinal abstractions, but living and longing for what he called "the marrow of the gospel." It was all about doing, not about believing ideas to be true or false. He told us to "Preach the gospel at all times, and only when necessary use words."

Francis made the following of Jesus something joyful and adventurous, not dour and moralistic. This is exactly what I have seen in so many of my Mennonite friends—and in their music too. It is all about orthopraxy (actual lifestyle) for them, instead of our usual mainline obsession with "orthodoxy," which far too often has been a mere cover for grossly self-serving and materialistic world views. Too much concern for being verbally and morally "right" has produced the exact opposite in too many Christians, it seems to me.

Mennonites seem to stumble along—sort of convinced they are half wrong and outside the mainstream of culture and academia—which ironically puts them at the structurally perfect and preferred place of the gospel! They prove what I have always believed and seen to be true: It is not that you "get" the Christian message and then people hate you and persecute you (which often merely strengthens the ego), so much as that the very state of exclusion, persecution, and failure allows you to actually get the gospel and forms of spirituality flowing naturally from it.

The early history of persecution by both Catholics and mainline Protestants got the Mennonites off to a good start. They knew that you could be quite "Christian" and still hateful, violent, and in love with power instead of Jesus. It became their continual exit strategy from "the system" and their ongoing entrance strategy into continuing growth, patience, humility, service, and gospel love.

That's the way I see it, anyway. But read this inspiring book, and you will know how Gordon Houser sees it—which is much better.

—*Richard Rohr, O.F.M.*
  Center for Action and Contemplation
  Albuquerque, New Mexico

Preface

Present

This book tries to pay attention to language, so let's begin by attending to the title. The first word of the title presents (pun intended) many meanings. *Webster's Dictionary* (11th. ed.) lists four categories, each with multiple definitions:

> (1) noun: a gift, something presented; (2) verb: to introduce someone or something to others; to make a gift to; to give or bestow formally; to bring before the public (as in a court of law); to nominate; to show or bring to one's attention; to perform; to aim, point or direct so as to face something or in a particular direction; (3) adjective: now existing or in progress, being in view or at hand, constituting the one at hand or being considered, constituting a verb tense expressive of present time or the time of speaking; (4) noun: the present words or statements, the present tense of a language, the present time (now).

Okay, many of you are not into reading dictionary definitions (which, by the way, I've shortened). I realize I'm odd ("differing markedly from the normal or ordinary or expected") in that I enjoy exploring language.

Along the way, I'll interject elements of my life story or experience. This provides a way for you to understand where I'm coming from, my bias, my point of view. It also acknowledges that we come to a topic, to a book (whether as readers or as the writer), with certain biases or assumptions that have developed out of our experiences.

So here's one of mine: Toward the end of my five-year college career (at four different schools) I decided to major in linguistics, which is the study of language. I began college interested in forestry. Soon I realized that interest had more to do with a love of the outdoors and romantic inclinations about nature than the nitty-gritty of caring for and measuring the potential board feet of trees. I transferred to a Bible college, where I fell in love with the study of Scripture.

My poor father, who with each change of school (and major) asked me, "What are you going to do with that?" He had come of age during the Depression, when you clawed for whatever job you could find. He had no luxury of choosing a career. Now here I was, pursuing something useless. Did I want to be a minister? he asked. No. I just enjoyed learning about the Bible—its meaning, history, and how it might be useful in living life.

After a year and a half, when a new school president came to power and wanted to enforce belief and restrict freedom of study, half the faculty and half the student body (including me) left. I transferred to Wichita (Kan.) State University. I had to declare a major if I was to graduate. I had studied New Testament Greek (called *koiné*) and found I loved language study. WSU offered a major in linguistics, so I chose that.

What? my father wondered. But by now he had given up my getting a degree in something useful. He just wanted me to get a degree, something he had not had the opportunity to obtain.

The linguistics program involved taking courses in various departments: English (where it was housed), psychology, philosophy, sociology, and foreign languages. This appealed to my eclectic interests and showed that language is at the heart of many disciplines. To these I would add the study of Christian spirituality, which is, I suppose, the category under which the book you're reading falls.

All of which is to say that I come with a love of language and a conviction about its importance in understanding one another and in living meaningful lives as Christians. Though I'm not a theologian, I like Gerald O'Collins' definition: "A theologian is someone who watches their language in the presence of God."

Let's go back to those definitions of "present." The title uses the word in the sense of definitions three and four, specifically the present tense of a language. But this book explores other meanings as well, including gift, the presence of a Person, and the present time—now.

I love to play with language (just ask my friends and colleagues who groan at my puns), and I encourage not only clarity but multiple meanings and connotations of words. So if you see the word *present* and drift off into memories of an early birthday present (I think of my first bicycle) that was of particular importance to you, I will not be disappointed. Or if you think of *campesinos* in a Salvadoran village who remember friends and relatives killed by paramilitary (or military) men and call out when hearing their names, *Presente!*—I will not be disappointed. Better yet, if these various connotations combine with the idea of (and the desire to practice) living in the present, I will be glad.

Tense

Webster's offers three categories in defining "tense":

(1) noun: a distinction of form in a verb to express distinctions of time or duration of the action or state it denotes; (2) adjective: stretched tight, feeling or showing nervous tension, marked by strain or suspense; (3) verb: to make tense.

Ostensibly, the word in the title adopts the first definition above and comes from grammar (which I enjoy). However, as with "present," I have multiple meanings and connotations in mind.

I hope in this book to address the tension many of us feel in our lives. Such tension arises from the many demands on our time and attention, the frenetic pace of life in our society, the bombardment of media—much of it calling us to participate in a deadening consumerism, purchasing products we don't need. This tension affects us physically, psychologically, and spiritually (more on that term later). It creates conflicts both internal and external.

I also hope to address the dynamic tension of living between opposite poles of belief and action. Another tension is between acknowledging what is, how things are, and encouraging change for the better. Related to this is the attempt to be descriptive and prescriptive (more on that under "Mennonite").

In my work as an editor I pay attention to how writers use tense. A basic rule is to be consistent. Some writers flit between past tense and present tense without realizing it. And reporters often use past tense without establishing a time for the event. Such inattention to tense can create confusion in the reader—or at least can hinder clarity. If she "said" something, when did she say it? If she "says" it, then it must be an ongoing option.

Tense applies as well to how we live our lives. Do we live with regret or nostalgia, wishing we could go back either to change an occurrence or to enjoy it? Or do we live in longing for a future when things will be better? Or do we worry about what will happen?

This book calls us (I include myself) to live as fully as we can in the present tense. I hope to explore why that is so difficult and how we might do that better.

A

The shortest word in the title—and the most common—is perhaps the most significant. This simple, one-letter article is both limiting and delimiting. It is only one yet one of many possible ones.

This book represents *a* (not *the*) Mennonite spirituality. It is my observation and opinion. It offers my limited perspective.

Mennonites who read this will at points recognize what I describe but at many points will say, No way. That's not true.

This is significant for at least three reasons.

First, it indicates that "Mennonite" refers to a variegated, complex group of people who practice their spirituality in many, various ways. While I contend there are characteristics that apply to most Mennonites, none of them applies to all Mennonites.

Second, it shows that this is one person's point of view. It hints at the postmodern perspective that we come to texts—either as readers or as creators—from our specific points of view. My take will not be the same as another's. This begs the question, Who am I to write such a book? It's merely an offering from one who has observed the wider Mennonite church for more than thirty years as a journalist while also being actively involved in a Mennonite congregation.

Third, I hope this "a" demonstrates one important aspect of Mennonite spirituality: *humility*, an imprecise word. I'm neither a sociologist nor a holy person. I'm just another voice. And I hope it's not a pretentious or preachy voice but instead a confessional one. As I'll say in more detail later, Mennonites have a knack for humility but don't do confession well. And, as I'll also explain later, both humility and confession are closely followed by their conniving twin: pride. Drawing attention to our humility or confession of sin is not a mark of holiness but a trait of our celebrity culture. You'll soon learn I'm no celebrity and don't have much to say that is titillating.

Why write it then? In short, as the scorpion said to the Buddhist monk that carried it across the river to safety before it stung him, It's what I do.

Mennonite

Many Mennonites have had an experience like this: You meet a stranger, perhaps your seatmate on a flight, and as you chat, the person learns you call yourself a Mennonite. The person gives you a quizzical look, and you rehearse your explanation of why you are on a plane instead of in a buggy and wearing chinos and a polo shirt instead of black pants, suspenders, and a wide-brimmed straw hat.

Perhaps you begin by downplaying the distinctions you're secretly proud of, saying, "Mennonites are Christians and live like everyone else," which is more true than you want it to be, since Mennonites are supposed to be different, to live exemplary lives. You mention that Mennonites believe in peace (maybe you even say you're pacifists) and in community. You also believe in voluntary church membership and thus adult baptism. All this while you're watching the other person for signs of boredom because you don't want to appear boastful (though secretly you do want to boast) and you don't want to appear coercive, which would go against your beliefs.

If the person does look bored, you stop talking, though you feel hurt because being Mennonite is important to you. At heart, it's more important than being (to get personal) a film buff, a KU (Kansas University) basketball fan, a Democrat, or a listener of Sixties pop music, especially the Beatles, though these would be more understandable to the person you're talking to.

Mennonites, like many people, I imagine, love to discuss their identity. Whenever the magazine I work for publishes an article on what it means to be Mennonite, we're sure to get several letters, each offering a different take on this important topic. And though humility is one trait most Mennonites agree is crucial, we're pretty self-centered. We even divide the world into Mennonites and non-Mennonites, though we make up less than 0.016 percent of the world's population. But I imagine Baptists, Catholics, Methodists, Pentecostals, and Presbyterians do the same thing.

If that person on the plane shows interest in learning more about Mennonites, you may refer to the beginning of your group in sixteenth-century Europe. You may explain that Mennonites got their name from an ex-Catholic priest in the Netherlands named Menno Simons, who helped galvanize Anabaptists after the debacle at Münster. Now you have to explain that Anabaptists—so named because they believed people should choose to be baptized, and since every citizen of the state was baptized into the state church, being baptized as an adult meant they were "baptized again" (the meaning of Ana-baptist)—broke away not only from the Roman Catholic Church but from Luther, Zwingli, Calvin, and other Reformers because they believed the church should be a voluntary association, not state-controlled, and thus that members of the church joined by voluntary baptism. They also believed that followers of Jesus Christ should not "wield the sword" against anyone, even enemies of the state (which was also the church, Catholic or Protestant), which at that time were the feared Turks.

Such beliefs did not endear them to state-church authorities, particularly when they acted on those beliefs by not baptizing their infant children (and thus reducing the number of people on the tax rolls). And refusing to fight the Turks was treasonous. So the authorities tried to stop this growing movement by arresting and often killing its followers—a few at first, then more and more. But the more they killed, the more people joined the movement. "Anabaptist" was a pejorative name given them by those who opposed them. They called themselves "*nachfolgen Christi*" (followers of Christ), since they saw that no one could truly know Christ unless they followed him in life. (More on that in Chapter One.)

If you've gotten this far, your seatmate is either unusually curious or too nice to turn away and read his or her book. For now, I'll end this imagined scene and simply address you, dear reader. If you are not acquainted with Mennonites, perhaps you'll find it interesting. If you are a Mennonite or acquainted with them, perhaps you'll want to argue with my description.

To return briefly to Mennonites' origins in the Anabaptist movement, let me caution that this movement, according to Mennonite scholar C. Arnold Snyder, "was a spontaneous, decentralized, grass-roots, underground movement of spiritual renewal and biblical reform, carried forward by 'common people' of no particular theological expertise" (*Following in the Footsteps of Christ: The Anabaptist Tradition*).

This reflects a theme of this book, that though I present a fairly simple approach to practicing Mennonite spirituality, that spirituality is complex, as is the world in which we live it out.

A turning point in this amorphous movement occurred in 1534, nine years after the movement's recognized beginning in

1525. Anabaptists in Münster, Germany, used violent measures to try to establish a kingdom and overthrow the local authorities. They proclaimed Münster the "new Jerusalem," and many Anabaptists flocked there, believing Christ's kingdom was about to be established. However, the local Catholic bishop organized an armed force that laid siege to the town. Finally, on June 25, 1535, the bishop's army gained entrance, and in the ensuing battle, many Anabaptists were killed, and their leaders were captured, tortured and displayed (see *Through Fire and Water: An Overview of Mennonite History*).

After Münster, persecution of Anabaptists increased. Menno Simons, a Catholic priest in Holland, joined the movement and helped return it to its earlier ideals and distinguish it from the violence at Münster. These peaceful Anabaptists were later called "Mennists," and still later Mennonites. Eventually the Swiss and South German Anabaptists adopted that name as well. Menno wrote extensively and greatly influenced the burgeoning movement.

Over the next several centuries, Mennonites moved around Europe until they found places of refuge from persecution. In the late seventeenth and eighteenth centuries, German and Swiss Mennonites migrated to America and settled in Pennsylvania. Others found a haven in Catherine's Russia, where they could live in peace, grow their Turkey Red wheat, and not face conscription into the army. Eventually Russia changed its mind, however, and in the 1870s, many of these "Russian Mennonites" (though German-speaking) migrated to America and settled in Kansas. Later, some of these moved north, stopping to reside in Nebraska, South Dakota, and Manitoba, Canada. Other immigrations occurred in the twentieth century, particularly in the 1920s and 1940s.

Besides the Bible, one of the most important and popular books for Mennonites has been *Martyrs' Mirror*, a massive collection of early Christian and Anabaptist martyr stories. Originally written in Dutch, it was later translated into German, then English and many other languages. These stories of martyrs (the word means witnesses) have had a profound effect on Mennonite identity. They've reinforced Mennonite beliefs in "nonresistance" (more on that in Chapter Three), offering examples of people who remained faithful to Christ and died rather than fight back. This experience also likely reinforced Mennonites becoming *die Stille im Lande* (the quiet in the land). They tended to migrate to places where they could live peacefully, do their work and not bother anyone.

Today, Mennonites who want to promote evangelism and mission decry this trait, calling it an unhealthy timidity. Beginning around the turn of the twentieth century, however, Mennonites did embark on missions, with workers going to India, China, and Native American tribes. More than a century later, Mennonites are growing fastest in Africa, South America, and Asia. In fact (and I usually try to get this into the conversation with my seatmate), the country with the second largest number of Mennonites is the Republic of Congo, and Ethiopia is moving up quickly.

So Mennonites are diverse, living in all parts of the world and practicing their faith in a variety of ways.

Webster's eleventh edition calls a Mennonite "a member of any various Protestant groups derived from the Anabaptist movement in Holland and characterized by congregational autonomy and rejection of military service." Despite the limitations of this, it's better than some older dictionary definitions that call Mennonites a "sect," which makes Mennonites cringe almost as much as that word's near homonym, "sex." Like other churches or denominations, Mennonites do not see themselves as schismatic, extreme, or heretical, part of the dictionary's definition of "sect." Instead they see themselves reflecting more faithfully than most the teachings of Christ. I suppose most members of any religious group feel their group is the most faithful; otherwise they'd leave.

Snyder and others argue that Anabaptists were neither Catholic nor Protestant but developed distinct beliefs and practices. An early Hutterite document noted that "Luther and

Zwingli exposed all the deception and villainy of the pope, . . . but they put nothing better in its place."

Today, Mennonites are in conversations with Catholics and Lutherans, who have apologized for killing Anabaptists (though the Augsburg Confession still damns them). And many Mennonites are learning from and being influenced by other Christian groups (more on that later), and these groups are often attracted to Mennonites' long peace tradition.

All of which is to say that the term *Mennonite* has definite characteristics yet is also fluid, ever changing.

Why do I use "Mennonite" instead of "Anabaptist" in my title? The short answer: I call myself a Mennonite and am most familiar with that group. Anabaptists include other groups (Brethren, Hutterites, and others) with which I'm less familiar. Some Mennonites prefer the term *Anabaptist* because Mennonite carries ethnic identity overtones. Then again, some who hear the word *Anabaptist* ask, "What you got against Baptists?"

I also use Mennonite broadly at times (there are more than a million in the world, from ninety-five denominations). Yet I am most familiar with my denomination, Mennonite Church USA, which is the largest Mennonite denomination and diverse in its own way. Still, it is also limited in its viewpoint and experience. I don't write out of the context of Congolese or Colombian or Chinese Mennonites, though I feel kinship with them and may refer to their experience. I write as an American, a white male with some education. So I come to the page from a position of privilege. But I also come as a Mennonite.

Spirituality

Okay, I admit it: While "spirituality" is overused, misunderstood, and used in wildly different ways, it looks cool in a title. But it's also an important concept that can help us live out our Christian practice and follow the way of the Spirit (one meaning of the word).

Many fine writers have eloquently addressed the meaning of "spirituality." Let me mention three—a Catholic, an evangelical, and a Mennonite, respectively.

Richard J. Woods calls spirituality "the intrinsic, self-transcending character of all human persons and everything that pertains to it, including, most importantly, the ways in which that perhaps infinitely malleable character is realized concretely in everyday life situations" (from *Christian Spirituality: God's Presence Through the Ages*). This is a mouthful, not least due to that pretentious word "persons," which people (not persons) love to use. But the point he makes is a good one: that spirituality is an aspect of everyone and shows up in everyday life. It's not some airy-fairy bliss or something only done on your yoga mat to the scent of incense or while sitting in a church or temple. Later he says it is "primarily concrete and real." I like that.

Woods also draws out "spirit" from the word, which he says refers to "the essential human capacity to receive and transmit the life of God, our unlimited openness to being, life and conscious relationship." In a footnote he quotes William Stringfellow about the holistic nature of spirituality: "Biblical spirituality encompasses the whole person in the totality of existence in the world, not some fragment or scrap or incident of a person."

Eugene H. Peterson prefers "spiritual theology," which he describes as "the attention that we give to the details of living life on this way [the Jesus-revealed Way]. It is a protest against the theology depersonalized into information about God; it is a protest against theology functionalized into a program of strategic plan for God" (from *Christ Plays in Ten Thousand Places: A Conversation in Spiritual Theology*). In other words, spirituality is about living, not just thinking or strategizing.

The problem with popular spirituality, Peterson writes, is that everyone is left "to make up a spirituality that suits herself or himself." But leaving us on our own leaves us "prone to addictions, broken relationships, isolation and violence." Peterson adopts spiritual theology because "'spiritual' keeps 'theology' from degenerating into merely thinking and talking and writing about God at a distance. 'Theology' keeps 'spiritual' from becoming merely thinking and talking and writing about the feelings and thoughts one has about God." Spirituality, then, is to be lived and to connect with God's life among us.

C. Arnold Snyder writes that "in the Christian tradition the 'life of the spirit' has always been understood to extend beyond the 'inner-looking' activities of prayer, meditation and contemplation" (see *Following in the Footsteps of Christ*). He quotes Philip Sheldrake in describing such spirituality as "the whole of human life, viewed in terms of a conscious relationship with God, in Jesus Christ, through the indwelling of the Holy Spirit and within a community of believers." Thus the major traits of spirituality include the inner and outer lives of Christians—their contemplative and active lives—in the context of the Trinity and the Christian community.

I like the points these writers make. And when I use "spirituality," I'd like you to pay attention to the first half of the word, the first six letters: s-p-i-r-i-t. It refers to living in the Spirit, the Holy Spirit. It means following the leading of the Spirit. And remember that in the Bible, the word for "spirit" (*ruach* in Hebrew, *pneuma* in Greek) can be translated "breath" or "wind" as well. I will emphasize the importance of breath in our living spiritually. And wind will help us better understand the importance of letting be and being carried. (Be assured, I've lived my life in Kansas; I know about wind.)

Too many people place attention on the first three-fourths of the word, the first nine letters: s-p-i-r-i-t-u-a-l. That's not so bad, except they often equate that with "incorporeal," or non-body. This then leads too often to a denigration of the body as unimportant, an attitude more Gnostic than Christian. I'll say more about this later, but for now let me emphasize that we are not spirits trapped in bodies; we are bodies. God created the world and its creatures, including flesh, and God said, "It is good" (Gen. 1:31). Spirituality is about how we live as bodies, not how we escape our bodies.

To summarize, then, this book is about living in each moment amid the tensions within and around us, and it is one Mennonite's description of how Mennonites live their lives in the Spirit and a prescription of how they (and you) might better live their (your) lives in the Spirit.

Each page is penned prayerfully, in hope that you, dear reader, will ponder each page prayerfully.

—*Gordon Houser*
  Newton, Kansas

present
tense

Chapter One

Practice

No one can truly know Christ unless he follow him in life.
—Hans Denck

You're heard the admonition, "Practice what you preach."
Maybe you've said it—aloud or under your breath—to
someone you felt was being hypocritical. Or maybe you've heard
it addressed to you and winced at its sting. A common com-
plaint—or perhaps an excuse—of the nonreligious about religious people is that they're hypocrites.

No doubt many of us are. We talk about our ideals, but our
real lives don't match up. Most of the time, I imagine, it's not out
of ill intent. We try to live out what we believe, but we often fail.
Unfortunately many people question the beliefs—the ideals—
because they aren't being practiced. This may not be logical (the
ideals may still be true, even if they aren't lived out), but it is understandable.

We Mennonites tend to believe in the importance of practicing our faith. Less important is the preaching part. We aren't
always as comfortable talking about it. We'd rather pick up debris after a tornado than talk to strangers about what we believe.

A well-known story tells of a man going door to door, hand-
ing out tracts about salvation. This man comes to the house of
an Amish man and asks him, "Are you saved?" The Amish man
replies, "Don't ask me; I could tell you anything. Ask my neighbors."

In other words, we should be judged by our actions. If we say we believe we should love our neighbor as ourselves but fail to do so, then do we really believe it?

Mennonites tend to agree with the phrase, The proof is in the pudding, or, as Jesus said, "You will know them by their fruits" (Matt. 7:16, 20). Better to act than talk about acting.

We tend to be less comfortable with the command to "always be ready to make your defense to anyone who demands from you an accounting for the hope that is in you" (1 Pet. 3:15).

Some who admire Mennonites for this inclination to practice our faith encourage us to "preach what you practice." More people need to know about this faith. Such talk tends to leave us feeling secretly proud and smug and a little embarrassed because we suspect they don't really know us that well.

There are Mennonites who talk (or write) about their faith. And the growing numbers of Hispanic, Asian, African, and other non-European Mennonites in the United States are showing how to share our faith more vocally. This book, after all, is an example of such sharing.

Nevertheless, at the heart of Mennonite spirituality is this bias toward living out our faith. Hans Denck was an early Anabaptist leader who wrote and spoke out against a kind of nominal Christianity that claimed to know Christ but failed to follow Jesus' words or example. Knowing Christ, he emphasized, was a process, not a one-time declaration.

Think of any close relationship you've had. You come to know people more intimately as you spend time with them and act in accordance with them.

This flies in the face of the state church approach of baptizing infants to guarantee them a place in the church—and thus in heaven (though those churches teach a catechism and confirm that baptism at a later age). It also goes against the later evangelical emphasis on making a decision to "get saved" and thus be assured a ticket to heaven.

Certainly for the Anabaptists—and later the Mennonites— making a decision to follow Jesus (usually marked by baptism)

was important. But discipleship, learning what it means to follow Jesus, was (and is) equally important. And this learning (the
root meaning of discipleship) is done best in a community of
such followers (more on that in Chapter Four).

This idea of process or following Christ in life is inherent in
both basic meanings of "practice," that of an action and that of
repeating an action to get it right. Some (evangelicals, for example) may criticize this as the "salvation by works" Luther railed
against. But while that may be a motivation for certain individuals, it's not true of Mennonite spirituality in general.

Salvation, Mennonites believe, is a gift of God. It's not
something we earn by any work, whether that's giving to the
poor (something Jesus talked about) or saying a certain kind of
prayer to ask Jesus into our heart (something Jesus did not talk
about). We depend on God's grace.

Yet as God's creatures, made in God's image, we are to live
out the love that exists in the Trinity—Father, Son, and Holy
Spirit—by loving God with our heart, soul, mind and strength
and our neighbors as ourselves. Such love—the Great Commandment Jesus spoke of—requires a lifetime of learning. It requires practice.

The basic approach to this practice is what the early Anabaptists called *Gelassenheit* (see more in Chapter Two), which
can be translated from the German as self-surrender or yielded-
ness. It implies a resignation to God's will, self-denial, a willing-
ness to suffer. That describes Jesus, who emptied himself (Phil.
2:7) and gave himself up to God out of love for us. And we are to
imitate Jesus in this way. Such imitation does not come quickly
or easily but needs formation in a community of others practicing this as well as the power of the Holy Spirit.

Gelassenheit, or yielding to God, is for Mennonites not just
the way you get saved, accept Jesus, are born again or whatever
language you use to describe conversion. Instead it is the way we
are to live. We are to yield our lives to God (and to one another)
all the time, each moment. That, in essence, is the message of
this book.

Evangelicals and others who emphasize conversion likely do not disagree with this. Just as Mennonites do not disagree that conversion is important. It's a matter of emphasis.

Since I'm contrasting Mennonites and evangelicals (at least in terms of emphasis), let me acknowledge that many (probably most) Mennonites in the United States agree with the evangelical emphasis on getting saved. They repeat the creed that Jesus died for our sins and that we must believe in Jesus. They look and act like evangelicals until you scratch the surface a bit. Ask about peace (see Chapter Three), and you'll hear, "Of course we're pacifists," with perhaps the qualifier, "but we shouldn't interfere in the government's affairs." Or bring a natural disaster to their area (by which I mean within five states of their home), and you'll see them go to work bringing assistance to those affected.

Peace and service are part of the DNA of this body of believers. Again, this doesn't mean every Mennonite believes in peace and service or practices them. But being in that community (another part of the Mennonite DNA), they'll be familiar with them.

Claiming this about Mennonites does not mean other Christian groups do not practice peace and service or that Gelassenheit is not important to them. It does not mean that evangelicals do not emphasize discipleship. I'm asking, What's at the heart of Mennonite spirituality? What distinguishes Mennonites from other groups in their practice of living in the Spirit?

Let's go back to that distinction between practice and preaching, between acting on our faith and talking about it. Perhaps that's not entirely helpful. After all, talking is a way of practicing the faith. And the early Anabaptists certainly talked about their faith. But it all went together for them. Because of the widespread persecution of Anabaptists, they had to be careful what they said and to whom. But their actions spoke volumes, and some of their talking occurred as they were being tortured and put to death—drowned or burned at the stake. These martyrs bore witness (the meaning of martyr) by their courage in the face of death as well as their words. And killing them proved in-effectual. The movement kept growing.

Practice, then, refers to living out our beliefs and to the process of learning to live out those beliefs by keeping at it, try-ing to get better at it. And we do this not to save ourselves, which we can't do anyway, but to live faithfully as God's people, created to love as God loves. Ephesians 2:10 says it well: "For we are what [God] has made us, created in Christ Jesus for good works, which God prepared beforehand to be our way of life."

From rock 'n roll to fundamentalist to Mennonite

I came to the Mennonite faith after college, having grown up in a more secular environment, then "getting saved" after watching Billy Graham on TV and later getting involved in a more fundamentalist style of Christian faith. Part of what at-tracted me to Mennonites was that they emphasized following Jesus' teachings, particularly the Sermon on the Mount. I did not grow up in a faith community that had practiced that em-phasis for almost 500 years but came to this understanding through my study of Scripture and theology as well as through my experiences with various churches.

How did I move from secular to fundamentalist to Men-nonite? Let me recount the journey briefly, acknowledging that it's one person's interpretation of one person's journey—not par-adigmatic.

When people asked me what my religious background was growing up, I used to say, "Pagan Methodist," which is not fair either to pagans or Methodists. Now I often say, Rock 'n roll. Not that I was a musician but that some of my most intense yearnings or senses of transcendence occurred through songs I heard. In the 1960s and early 1970s, I listened to the Top 40 on the radio but soon began collecting albums of favorite artists, such as Simon and Garfunkel, Bob Dylan, the Beatles, and many others. When I use the phrase "senses of transcendence" about rock 'n roll, I don't mean I understood it that way at the time or that these artists were necessarily singing about God.

The music served to take me out of myself for a while and experience certain emotions or think about larger issues. It helped me sense an order or beauty beyond my mundane life.

When I was fifteen, I learned I had a growth deficiency in my lower vertebrae, which prevented my taking part in contact sports. I was entering high school that fall and hoped to excel at wrestling. Suddenly I had to give it up. I felt crushed, my dreams dashed. The following spring, after watching a broadcast of a Billy Graham crusade, I went to my room and gave my life to Jesus, using the words Graham suggested.

Nothing magical happened right away, but my life had a new focus, a new meaning and direction. I had a clear sense that certain things I did had to change. One notable change, apparent to my friends, was that I stopped taking part in telling racist jokes. I gave up racist remarks altogether and soon avoided the guy most involved in that behavior.

I didn't know other Christians or what it meant to be one. I attended church with my mother. My parents had all seven of their children (I'm the youngest) go to Sunday school at the First United Methodist Church in Emporia, Kansas, until we went through catechism—or whatever they called it. I remember going to a class on Saturday mornings, wishing I could be playing or watching cartoons, not liking it but knowing I should. After six weeks or so, we were either confirmed or baptized, and I remember wanting it to be meaningful, but I didn't really understand it all or feel fully invested in it. This happened a few years before my experience at age fifteen.

After my conversion, I read the Bible, figuring that was important, but I didn't understand it well. Once I read about Daniel and his friends refusing to eat meat (it was actually meat sacrificed to idols), and I thought I should become a vegetarian. I tried to stop eating meat, a staple at our house, but it only upset my mother, and I didn't explain well my reasons for it. I was reticent to talk about religion, partly because I couldn't articulate my beliefs well. It seemed more an instinct; I wanted to do right but wasn't always sure what that involved.

In my junior year, I joined some other students on a Vietnam War moratorium day in the spring. As I recall, I wore a black armband and signed a petition opposing the war. Doing so was partly an instinct that war is wrong (a good instinct, I now aver) and partly a desire to be involved with others in some larger cause.

In my senior year, I joined the school's Fellowship of Christian Athletes (my back allowed me to play tennis, the only sport I lettered in), but that only involved a few meetings. I also became active in an environmental action group in the school (another good instinct). But mostly I was a loner who studied, listened to music, played tennis, and had a few close friends. To one in particular, Brett, I confided my Christian beliefs. I looked for meaning in certain songs I thought might reflect my faith. I loved George Harrison's album *All Things Must Pass*, only admitting later that he was clearly espousing a form of Hinduism, but at least it was religious.

Once I arrived at college, attending Emporia State University my first year and living at home, I got involved in a local Baptist church and in Bible study groups with Christian friends I made. I learned more about the Bible, but the perspective of the church and the Bible study groups was fundamentalist, a description the church claimed proudly. Still, I'm in debt to that pastor and those friends for giving me loving care and a devotion to the Bible as the Word of God. And while many of my views about Scripture and faith have changed, it was partly their help in studying the Bible that allowed me to change those views.

In other ways my instincts as a young, untutored Christian proved truer than the teachings of that little Baptist church. I felt confused when the pastor emphasized patriotism and supporting the military. I even hung out our flag at home. I also recall a dinner the church put on for the young people (college and high school students, mostly). The guest speaker told some racist jokes in his speech. I felt appalled and confused.

When I turned eighteen, I had to register for the draft (this was 1971). I wanted to register as a conscientious objector, but when I told my parents, they were shocked. All three of my older bothers had already been in the military, two in the army and one in the National Guard. One brother had survived a year in Vietnam, though he came back changed. My parents said they didn't want me to get drafted necessarily, but to be a CO was unacceptable. My mother cried, and my father said he was ashamed of me. I had five days to decide, and after much prayer I decided to give up applying as a CO. (I probably wouldn't have received it anyway.) I told my mother my decision and said I'd been praying about it. She said she had been praying, too.

I was registered 1-A, and my name entered the draft lottery the following spring. I called the afternoon birthdays were drawn, and I waited, tense, knowing my future direction, perhaps my life, lay in the number I was about to hear. The voice said that my birthday, August 22, was the 140th date selected. My body sagged in relief. The understanding then was that only numbers up to 100 would likely be drafted. I could continue my college education with confidence, if not certainty, that I would not be drafted.

A year later I enrolled in a Bible college in Kansas City, Missouri (see Preface), continuing my study of Scripture and theology in a concentrated way. The school was conservative, yet several of its teachers gave me tools to study the Bible for myself and come to my own views about it. My New Testament professor, Dr. Hoch, once told our class in First Corinthians that he was not there to tell us what to think about Scripture but how to study it.

I spent a year and a half there, then left, along with nearly half the student body and half the faculty, when a new president took over the school's leadership and basically demanded that teachers indeed tell us what to think. As it happened, I needed to leave anyway, since I could no longer afford it. This private school cost three times the tuition at a public university, and I was paying my own way, working full-time in summers and half-time (when I could find jobs) during the school year. (And I didn't want to borrow money.)

The day I left that school, following a May term in which I took Greek 3, my parents' '69 Chevy Nova loaded with my belongings—clothing and books—a tornado hit my hometown of Emporia. I turned on the car's radio as I left Kansas City that Saturday afternoon and heard a news report that a tornado had struck Emporia and was headed northeast, toward Kansas City. Having grown up in Kansas, I was used to hearing about tornadoes, but I was not accustomed to hearing about them hitting my town and heading toward me.

I drove through heavy rain, had to pull over once because the rain was so intense that I couldn't see beyond fifty feet. I kept thinking, *Is my family okay? Will I be okay?* Eventually I learned that the tornado hit the west side of the town. My parents lived on the east side. When I reached their house, they weren't home, and the door was locked. I drove to my brother's house a few miles away. He was at work, but the door was unlocked. I went inside. Soon the tornado sirens went off. He had no basement, so I tipped over his couch and lay under it. After some tense minutes, the sirens stopped.

My parents returned home, and I unloaded my car and spent the night there. The next day, I had my first encounter with Mennonites. I drove that morning to an area of town on the west side where the tornado had damaged some houses. I saw about twenty people picking up debris, working steadily and quietly, most of them middle-aged. I wondered if they were local, though I didn't recognize any of them. I set to work near a woman who was probably twice my age (I was twenty at the time) and who seemed to know what she was doing. After a while, I asked where she was from, and she mentioned a town I cannot recall. (For all I know, she was from Newton, my current residence.) She smiled and said she was with Mennonite Disaster Service (MDS). I expected her to go into some speech about why her group was so important and try to convince me to join them (I'd had run-ins with Moonies and other groups and done my own proselytizing), but she soon stopped talking and kept working.

I thought, *Wow, these people are here this soon from many miles away, helping strangers.* Emporia had no Mennonite churches. I left after several hours, tired. They were still working.

In this book I'm dealing partly with generalities, looking for ways to typify Mennonite spirituality. Here's one: physical, practical work that serves others. It's fitting—and not unusual—that my first encounter with Mennonites was in helping clean up after a tornado. Such a scene could serve as an icon of Mennonite spirituality: men and women in blue jeans and work shirts, wearing gloves, maybe a hat to protect from the sun, using a hammer (one of the symbols used for MDS) to pull nails from boards or to knock loose boards that can then be piled up and hauled away. This captures Mennonites at their best and most comfortable: busy with practical work, away from church and not required to talk to others about religion. And they get to feel good (and proud) about helping others, much preferable to having to be a recipient of such aid.

I'm not as comfortable in that scene, though I've been there. As recently as 2007, I spent a day helping clean up debris in and around Greensburg, Kansas, after a tornado leveled much of that town. I was there for one day and glad to return home to a shower and rest. Many people and groups volunteer to help victims of such natural disasters, but MDS has been doing this a long time (since 1950) and has volunteers there for the long haul, sometimes for years afterward, to help residents get back into their houses and on their feet.

I'm glad they do it, but I prefer more comfortable work that involves reading and writing. Thus, I'm still in some ways an outsider observing these people from my rock 'n roll upbringing, amazed at their sense of service passed down from one generation to another.

While that sense of service is strong, it is changing, not least in how it is demonstrated. While many young people volunteer to serve in this way, a disproportionate number of such volunteers are retired or are older than fifty.

When I mentioned to my spiritual director (a Mennonite pastor in his forties) this representative image of Mennonites helping after a natural disaster, he noted that such an image does not fit young adult Mennonites (say, under thirty) today. He said he isn't sure what image would fit—and neither am I. There is a Bike Movement that consists of young Mennonites riding bikes around the United States, Canada, and even Asia to raise awareness of Mennonite World Conference, a communion of Mennonite bodies around the world. Many young Mennonites join one of the church's voluntary service programs. Some in my area are into organic gardening. But no overriding image fits.

Another image, particularly of older Mennonite women, is that of a quilting circle. Many still piece quilts and donate them to relief sales organized by Mennonite Central Committee, a relief and development organization that serves in ninety-five countries around the world. These circles combine Mennonite virtues of practical service and community. Add in another virtue of simplicity, reusing discarded material to create a quilt, and you have a trifecta.

I would add here a virtue Mennonites don't always acknowledge but present nonetheless: beauty. While these quilts serve practical purposes—the chief one being the money they raise to help those in need—the people who buy them at the relief sales do so not for their warmth but for their beauty. I would further argue—in fitting with the major point of this book—that beauty exists not only in the finished product but in the act of sewing together the pieces. These women (I'm sure there are men who do this as well, but the vast majority of Mennonite quilters are women) make a difficult task look easy as they sew while talking. There is a beauty in such skill being practiced in a quiet rhythm.

Both in quilting and in cleaning up debris and repairing houses, these Mennonites exhibit the kind of mindful practice in the present that I long to do and that can put us in touch with the presence of God's Spirit in our lives. I've observed such people doing their tasks unselfconsciously, focusing on the work at hand.

Such practice reflects aspects of Mennonite spirituality and touches a profounder aspect of Christian spirituality—living fully in each moment, aware less of self than of being in God's presence.

This gets tricky, both semantically and practically. Being aware of our living in the present is part of the practice (in the sense of repetition until we get it right) that can lead to the practice (actually doing it) of living in the present unselfconsciously.

At once

Living in the present is at once the easiest and the hardest thing you'll do. And the key is found in those two short words (six letters) *at once.*

That, in fact, is where we live, even if we often (most of the time, an interesting expression) do not realize it. "At once" describes a moment and implies a union of disparate elements. Another term we use is "the present"—or now.

Living there, in the now, is easy because it's where we live— without any required effort. Realizing that is the hard part. "Realizing" has to do with what's real. To realize something is, in a sense, to make it real. But in reality (another interesting term), realizing means becoming aware of something real.

It can also carry the meaning of attainment. We might say, "She realized her potential when she won the race." She attained what had been unrealized. Then it became real. It happened.

How then do we realize (make real) the reality that we live at once, in the present? This leads to another question, Why should we care?

Before we answer these, let's look back at the easy and hard parts of living in the present.

Easy

We exist, we breathe. Those are gifts from our Creator. As gifts, they signify grace. We are alive through no effort of our own. And we breathe usually without thinking about it (asthmatics and others, such as my father in the last several years of

his life, dependent on a machine that fed him oxygen, may disagree). We live through each moment by God's grace.

Difficult

Receiving that gift of life with gratitude and awareness is not
automatic. That takes some effort, what I call practice. Such
awareness of the gift of life and breath is more intense (or present) when that gift seems threatened. When our breathing is la-
bored or when our life feels fragile, we may stop and think (or
feel): Yes, thank you, God, for life.

The trick (it's not a trick but straightforward) is how to be
aware and grateful without requiring extenuating circumstances, such as illness or danger. There is no magic formula. It
requires practice.

Better, practices. And there are many. Let me mention a few:

Breathing

While this generally occurs routinely, try doing it slowly,
rhythmically. For example, sit still and inhale through your
nose, letting your diaphragm expand, then exhale through your
mouth, letting your diaphragm deflate. This has a calming effect
and helps your body relax, but it also helps you be more aware of
your breathing, that gift from God, and thus helps you live in
the present, and thus in reality.

Thanksgiving

A frequent theme in Scripture and the most common form
of prayer in the Bible is giving thanks. Take time (another interesting expression) to verbalize your thanks to God for life. Add
other gifts as well. David Stendl-Rast is a good guide here. You
can offer thanks in words, aloud or silent, in song, in gesture or
simply. You can combine it with your breathing, thanking God
for the miraculous way your body functions, all the many parts
that work together in such a way that you are alive. Thanking
God for this moment may feel easy when relaxing, say, beside a
mountain stream or watching a beautiful sunset. But when in

discomfort or pain or in a tense moment when several sources demand your attention it can feel difficult, to say the least.

Slowing down

Such practices require time, which our culture tends to view as a rare commodity. We rush from one activity to another, usually thinking about two or three other activities we'd like to be doing (or rather, getting done). We live in a world of quantification, where product is valued over process, quantity over quality. To slow down and give our attention to breathing, to giving thanks or to a dozen daily tasks—cooking, washing dishes, brushing our teeth, getting dressed, you name it—is a countercultural exercise. And while Mennonites may take pride in being countercultural, speed is engrained in our psyches. We like to get things done. We are rewarded—paid money, given praise, feel good, that we have a purpose—when we accomplish things. In this way, Mennonites tend to be good Americans—practical, utilitarian.

Slowing down, then, is a requirement for living in the present but also difficult to do. It takes practice, doing it over and over until it becomes almost natural.

My physical therapist has told me about muscle memory. If you do a certain activity 500 times, the muscles used for that activity respond almost automatically when you begin it.

My daughter ran hurdles in high school and college. She had to learn the technique of going over each hurdle as low and as quickly as she could. She got the basic technique down, but to improve on her time she had to keep refining her technique. And she had to keep practicing so that her hurdling became automatic. The more she had to think about it, the worse she performed.

Living in the present, like any spiritual discipline, requires practice. It involves trying and failing, then trying again. It also requires motivation, believing it is worth doing.

I could argue that such a practice will make you happier and more serene, and I believe it will. But such a tack reflects American consumerism more than it reflects biblical obedience. And you don't live in the present by thinking how it will help you in the future. Ends-means thinking is antithetical to living in the moment.

I won't argue that such a practice will get you saved or a reward in heaven. But I will invite you to look to Jesus, who lived this practice, aware that he lived and served in the presence of God the Father. And though he healed many and taught the crowds and his disciples many truths, his was no assembly line operation. He didn't even begin his "ministry" until he was around thirty (What kind of productivity is that?), and he often retreated to a deserted place to pray. Finally, in a most un-utilitarian fashion, he gave himself up to his enemies to be killed.

Jesus lived in the reality of God's presence. He participated in the trinitarian love that is eternal (ever present). As creatures made in God's image, we, too, are made to live in that eternal love. We are directed to love God with our heart, soul, mind and strength—and our neighbors—not for some future reward but because that is who we are created to be.

It's the ultimate realism. Living "at once" is easy and hard. It is following Jesus each moment and receiving forgiveness—over and over—as we fail.

More than two years after meeting those Mennonites on that Sunday morning in an Emporia yard, I joined a Mennonite congregation and thus became a Mennonite. By then I had studied Scripture, theology, and church history on my own and decided that's where I belonged. But I still didn't know what I was getting into. I'm still learning.

Chapter Two

Patience

I waited patiently for the Lord. —Psalm 40:1

Perhaps you've been in a situation like one of these: You're in a car on a hot summer day, stuck in traffic that's moving at a snail's pace. You are due at a doctor's appointment perhaps. Or you want to get home to make supper before you have to be at an evening meeting. You long for the traffic to part like the Red Sea for Moses and drive on unimpeded. Your blood pressure rises. Your muscles tense. You feel the urge to scream. You do not love the people in the other cars and trucks (most of them vision-blocking SUVs or large pickups) that sit in your way. Why do they have to be on the road now?

Or you're at the grocery store, where you've stopped on the way home from work to pick up a few items you need for supper. You have just enough time to rush home, prepare the meal, and get to your evening meeting. You get in the shortest checkout line you find, one that says fifteen items or less (should say fewer). The man ahead of you has a cart with twenty-six items (you count them). You do not love this man. You want to confront him, complain to the checker or the manager, but that would only prolong your stay. Then after the checker announces the total, the woman ahead of him pulls out a checkbook. You want to yell, "Why didn't you have the check filled out except for the amount ahead of time?" You do not love this woman.

Or you arrive at the airport to check in. You are scheduled to be in Chicago for a meeting that afternoon, and your flight should arrive in plenty of time to take the El downtown and walk a few blocks to your hotel. (You're a Mennonite and committed to saving money; otherwise you might take a cab.) You discover that your flight is delayed because of weather. What? You've just come in from bright sunshine. The board says it is delayed an hour. I can still make it, you tell yourself. An hour later you learn the flight is cancelled. You join a line of people trying to book alternative flights. You do not love these people. Why are so many of them flying? You do not love the ticket agent, who tells you the only flight out is at 3:30 p.m., after your meeting has started. Your muscles tense. You want to scream.

I could go on, no? We live in a fast-paced world that lives by the rules of what Carl Honoré calls "a cult of speed" (see *In Praise of Slowness: Challenging the Cult of Speed*). The chief rule is, Do everything faster. We have succumbed to what Dr. Larry Dossey calls "time-sickness." This frenetic pace of life affects our health, our relationships, our faith. Living in what Honoré calls "the age of rage," we find it difficult to love—others, our families, ourselves.

If the greatest commandment of our Lord is to "love the Lord your God . . . and your neighbor as yourself," how do we do that while racing from one task to another and resenting everyone who gets in our way?

Honoré's book describes this addiction to speed and the Slow Movement that tries to address it. This worldwide movement has risen out of frustration with the effects of our fast-paced lifestyles, particularly in the West. He writes about people applying slowness to cities, exercise, medicine, sex, work, leisure, and raising children. Slowing down, however, requires more than merely changing structures or creating new rules. It requires changing ourselves, learning to feel comfortable with slowness.

I've been as addicted as most people to the cult of speed. Back in the early 1980s I worked with a colleague, Larry Cornies, who was one of the most laid-back people I'd met. He joked with me about my Type A behavior, how I had a hard time doing just one thing at a time. When I watched TV, I had to have a book or magazine with me and try both to read and watch, doing neither well. Or if I had to wait in line—at a theater or ball game, say—I carried a book with me to read.

To me, this behavior wasn't weird or sick; it made perfect sense. I thought, *What a waste of time to just stand there doing nothing when I can get a few pages read!* Being an introvert, talking to people was not appealing. And being addicted to reading and aware of the many books I wanted to read but never got to, it seemed reasonable to use every available minute to read whatever I could.

Among the books I read were ones on prayer, on living in the present moment. I knew this was important, yet my addiction frustrated my attempts to do so. Another factor was (is) my inclination toward life, how I operate in the world.

Myers-Briggs and the Enneagram

There are dozens, maybe hundreds, of systems for labeling and understanding how people approach life. Two I'm most familiar with are the Myers-Briggs Type Indicator and the Enneagram. These are imperfect ways to understand who we are, yet I find them helpful.

Sometime in the first decade of our marriage, Jeanne and I attended a class at a Mennonite church in town on the Myers-Briggs model. We took the test and figured out our types and how those interact. I came out pretty strongly an INTJ (I=introvert, N=intuitive or seeing the big picture more than the details, T=thinking, J=judging or tending to make decisions quickly and decisively instead of putting them off as well as craving structure). Jeanne, on the other hand, came out ESFJ (E=extrovert, S=sensing or seeing the details, F=feeling), and her J was not far on the continuum from a P, which stands for perceiving, or needing to process decisions longer than a J would and tending to be more spontaneous.

Besides confirming the adage that opposites attract, this exercise helped us understand each other better. Learning that extroverts draw energy from being with people, while introverts recharge themselves with time alone helped Jeanne understand why I needed some time by myself first thing in the morning. And we better understood one of our persistent conflicts, that while she saw all the things around the house that needed doing, I was focused on world crises or ideas from books I was reading or issues at church. Once she pointed out these details, I was willing to do the tasks. I just didn't usually notice them.

All of which is to say that we relate to the world in different ways and from different perspectives. The Myers-Briggs and other systems help us understand this without passing judgment. No type is better than another; it's just different.

The Enneagram is different in that it aims at change. One of the older typologies, it describes nine different character types (thus its name). But, as Richard Rohr and Andreas Ebert write in *The Enneagram: A Christian Perspective,* "it confronts us with compulsions and laws under which we live—usually without being aware of it—and it aims to invite us to go beyond them, to take steps into the domain of freedom."

Although it is complex, the Enneagram can help us identify our obsessions, our weaknesses, and our favorite sins while also pointing us toward wholeness. It fits well with the biblical idea of repentance, of turning from unloving, ego-centered living toward loving, other-oriented living. And that, as I said, is the main goal of our life: to love God and our neighbor as ourself.

I won't try to explain the Enneagram in detail. For that, read the above-mentioned book or any of dozens of others. But let me illustrate its use with my own experience.

After taking several different tests and reading some books, I'm pretty sure I'm a Five in the Enneagram typology. Fives are "head" people, drawn to knowledge, which is our main temptation, for knowledge is power. We tend to see ourselves as objective, able to see through things, and we try to avoid emptiness. The root sin of Fives is avarice or greed. We like to hoard things, especially knowledge. I collect books. We're drawn to explanatory systems like the Enneagram. The fact that I'm writing a

book that tries to explain Mennonite spirituality is a strong in-
dication that I'm a Five.

We tend to fear emotional engagement and defend ourselves from it by withdrawing into a world of ideas, for example.
Fives tend to take rather than give, and our pitfall is emotional
stinginess. Twos, which I'll explore later as typical of Mennonites as a whole, like to give. Perhaps this is another reason Jeanne
(who is a Two) and I came together.

Fives aren't all bad. Our greatest gifts are a reversal of our
obsessions, as Rohr and Ebert write: "They are contemplatively
gifted, they understand connections, they invent grand intellectual systems. Their main gift to the church is objectivity."

The gift and sin of Fives is detachment. "Fives are the only
type with which we can use the same word to describe their
greatest strength and greatest weakness," write Rohr and Ebert.
So when I use the word *detachment* or discuss attachment as a
problem, you'll understand my bias.

Understanding this and acknowledging my tendencies
helps me change and mature. The invitation to Fives is wisdom,
the kind that comes not just from thought but from real-life experience. Fives are drawn toward prayer and meditation, which
are sources of power, but we must learn to act. (When I described Mennonites in Chapter One as oriented toward practice
or service, I was mostly describing other Mennonites.)

Rohr and Ebert point to Dietrich Bonhoeffer (1906-1945)
as an example of a redeemed Five. A trained theologian and university lecturer, he became director of the illegal preachers' seminary of the Confessing Church in Germany at age twenty-nine.
After the Nazis banned him from teaching in 1936, he went to
America and was invited to stay. Instead he caught the last ship
back to Germany before the war broke out. In 1942, he joined
the circle that was planning Hitler's assassination, and in 1943
he was arrested. He spent two years in prison, then was hanged
on April 9, 1945. In prison he wrote, "Freedom is not in the
flight of thoughts but only in action." Not what you'd expect
from a Five.

I can write about spirituality, but to move toward wholeness and a more loving life, I must act, seek to live out that spirituality, not just think about it.

As I consider patience and my need to slow down, I must learn to act, to practice patience in my daily life.

But first, why patience? And what is it? "Patience," says Webster's, is "the capacity, habit or fact of being patient." And the adjective *patient* has four basic definitions: (1) bearing pains or trials calmly; (2) manifesting forbearance under provocation or strain; (3) not hasty or impetuous; (4) steadfast despite opposition, difficulty, or adversity. And I want to throw in the noun form, which refers to one awaiting or under medical care or other services and one that is acted upon.

That's the what. Why write a chapter on patience? Because it is a central virtue and concept in Mennonite spirituality. Behind patience lies the theological truth, the belief, that our life—all life—is a gift of God and that we are not in charge. To live ungratefully and act as if we are in charge, as if everything depends on us, is to be, among other things, impatient.

Gelassenheit

At the heart of being patient is the practice of *humility*, a weak word that carries connotations of servility and ignoring injustice. Early in their experience in Europe, Mennonites used the German word *Gelassenheit* to describe a basic approach to life as followers of Jesus. Sometimes translated "humility," this word has a fuller meaning (see Chapter One). Close to this is the Greek word *kenosis* (emptiness) as used in Philippians 2:7, which says that Jesus "emptied himself" and took on the form of a servant.

At the heart of Mennonite spirituality and ethics is the call to imitate Jesus our Lord. That does not mean wearing sandals and tramping through the Galilean countryside (though I suppose it could). And it doesn't primarily mean healing lepers and forgiving sinners, though it certainly could include that. Primarily we are to imitate Jesus in his act of giving himself to God, yielding his life, "even to death on a cross," rather than taking or acting as if he is in control. Taking the form of a servant means serving rather than ruling, healing rather than killing, forgiving rather than seeking revenge, and being patient rather than coercing and trying to take control.

The martyrs in Christian history are examples of such imitation of Jesus. But in many other, ordinary, daily ways we are to imitate Jesus by practicing Gelassenheit. While such practice may at times appear heroic and cause a sensation, such as the Amish community in Pennsylvania forgiving the man who murdered five Amish schoolchildren in 2005, it is mostly mundane. Doing our daily work honestly and faithfully; serving our spouse or friends; raising children with forbearance; going to one another in our church to raise concerns, confess wrongdoing or forgive; showing hospitality to people we know or to strangers. All these practices and more require small yet crucial decisions to relinquish control or expectations for how things should be. Gelassenheit means emptying ourselves of desires that may lead us to use power over others for our own ends.

This is never easy and requires continuous practice and the support and example of others to help form us into patient people. Such practices occur in thousands of ways. Here's one example:

Years ago we had neighbors with young children. The children enjoyed playing in the woods behind our house. We found damage to some of the trees, and one day Jeanne saw their oldest boy cutting the bark from a young walnut tree with a hatchet. She called out his name to talk to him, but he ran home. Jeanne went over to talk to his mother and showed her the damage to the tree. As they were talking, the woman's husband came out and soon berated Jeanne for interfering in their family. Besides, he said, these trees belong to everybody. Jeanne pointed out that actually the trees were on our property, and while we didn't mind their kids playing in the woods, we didn't want the trees damaged. He became more belligerent. Jeanne smelled alcohol on his breath and soon walked away.

When she told me what had happened, my anger rose. I did not think kind thoughts toward this man. I wanted to hurt him. I'm not one to attack others physically, especially since I'm the one likely to get hurt, but I thought of attacking him verbally or maybe calling the police. I felt protective of Jeanne yet also a bit helpless. A social worker (and a good one), she is more practiced in dealing with conflict than I. She told me my going over there wouldn't help. Once he was sober, he'd probably regret what he had done, she said.

Probably more out of fear than faith, I stayed put. I also felt a strong internal urge to pray for my neighbor. This seemed to be a case of praying for my enemy. (He is still on my prayer list these many years later.) The neighbor kids continued to play in the woods but stopped chopping on trees. I spoke with my neighbor at various times. These were friendly conversations, and nothing was said about the incident in the woods. My anger subsided, and our lives went on.

What I'm trying to describe is not a strategy but a practice that manifests itself in various ways, all reflecting patience. I pulled out one experience in which I stumbled onto this practice. I can name many in which I failed. I especially recall with sadness and regret the times I became angry at my children and lost patience with them. What patience I have I have learned largely from being around Jeanne and others, observing their responses to situations, and praying that I might learn from them.

Patience often means waiting. The word *wait* (in its various forms) occurs 144 times in the Protestant Bible. As in Psalm 40, God's people are often encouraged to wait for the Lord. Behind this command or practice lies the truth that God is the one in control. There are many ways throughout our day that we are called to act. But at times we are called to wait. To wait requires faith, and to practice waiting requires slowing down.

The gospel (good news)

This is clear in the gospel (good news) Jesus proclaimed. Mark tells us that following Jesus' baptism, his temptation in the wilderness and John's arrest, "Jesus came to Galilee, proclaiming the good news of God," which is this: "The time is fulfilled, and the kingdom of God has come near; repent, and believe in the good news" (Mark 1:14-15).

The good news is that God rules, God is in charge, and we are not. (A friend of mine likes to say her basic belief is, There is a God, and you're not him—or her.) To believe this—not just in our heads but to live as if this is true—we must repent. That word (*metanoia* in Greek) means to turn around, to walk in a different direction. The world around us pushes in the direction of acting as if we are in charge, in the direction of haste, of finding the quick solution, in the direction of getting things done, no matter what means are required.

Jesus' gospel calls us to turn away from the world's direction of haste and control; it calls us to slow down and wait for God, who is in charge, to act. Notice this gospel message says nothing about a personal relationship with Jesus or gaining entrance to heaven. This is good news because it names the reality that it isn't up to us. It is God's kingdom. We are to believe this. And belief, as I said, is not merely an intellectual assent but an ongoing practice of faithfulness, of living into this truth, waiting for the leading of the Holy Spirit before taking action. It means imitating Jesus, who proclaimed God's rule and lived its truth, all the while saying, "Not my will but yours be done."

We are to practice patience in an impatient world. This practice is the basis for making peace (see the next chapter) and requires formation in a community committed to listening to the Spirit and walking according to that leading (see Chapter Four).

Such waiting does not mean inaction or stasis. Like Fives on the Enneagram typology, we are called to act. But we act slowly, mindfully, not in desperation, as if everything depended on us. No, we act in faith and in faithfulness, thanking God for the gift of life and bearing patiently the suffering that comes, as we await the final justice and shalom that God will bring.

We learn patience as we live in the tension of God's rule, which has come and is not yet come in fullness. Another aspect is the tension between accepting what is real while pursuing the ideal. We work and yearn for God's justice to reign in every part of life—that the hungry find food, the sick healing, the oppressed freedom—yet we must acknowledge that injustice exists. And we believe—most Mennonites believe—that we only get to peace or justice by living peacefully or justly. The end does not justify the means.

A part of acknowledging the real is adjusting our expectations, which is difficult for those of us living comfortably in a wealthy country. In her book *Brokenness and Blessing: Towards a Biblical Spirituality*, Frances M. Young writes that the presupposition in our culture "is that bad things shouldn't happen, or certainly shouldn't happen to good people; and since they do happen and the world is imperfect, there cannot be a God." Our post-Enlightenment tendency is to see suffering as grounds for atheism.

"We live in a world of violence and conflict and pray for peace," Young writes. "We deplore suffering, injustice and poverty but live comfortably off the oppression of others." She calls us to "move beyond an easy spirituality of personal well-being, comfort and happiness to rediscover the wilderness way that lies at the heart of the Bible."

As a Five, I'd much prefer sitting in a comfortable recliner reading a good book to moving beyond comfort to the wilderness way. So Young speaks to me, not just to us.

The X-rated Bible

The Bible presents a God of love and ends with a new Jerusalem, where "death . . . mourning and crying and pain will be no more" (Rev. 21:4), yet it is refreshingly realistic about the suffering and injustice in the world. Its characters are flawed, capable of great goodness and great evil. Its songs and prayers express joy and praise as well as anguish and anger. I've written that if the Bible were a movie, it would be rated at least R, if not X.

Those of us who look to this text as God's Word to us and seek God's guidance through it too often romanticize its message and ignore its troublesome parts. Patience and Gelassenheit grow out of acknowledging the suffering around us and suffering ourselves. Accepting this reality keeps us humbly aware that we are not in charge. But we also must accept the reality that God is in charge. Such faith helps us endure suffering with hope rather than lashing out at others to try to control it.

I'm writing in broad, theological terms. But patience is personal. We all suffer to some degree, and we are most tested in our faith in such encounters. When I'm in pain (and I live with chronic pain from an auto accident in 1982), I want it fixed—now. Yet I've learned that to expect such a fix only increases the pain. Although the practice is centuries old in the Christian tradition (and in other traditions), a sports medicine doctor first encouraged me to face my pain (not deny its reality), live in the moment (not seek escape in the past, remembering a time before I had the injury that led to my pain, or the future, when it will be healed) and to give thanks for that moment.

This practice of being in the present moment with my pain and giving thanks is a form of contemplative prayer. Thomas Keating has explored what he calls "centering prayer" in his book *Intimacy with God: An Introduction to Centering Prayer*. It is a form of Gelassenheit, of yielding to what is rather than trying to fight it (and losing the battle). Call it a form of nonviolent resistance (more on that in the next chapter). Curiously, it is also effective. Relaxing and breathing slowly as I face my pain tends to diminish the pain. However, it doesn't get rid of it, and so I must practice this regularly.

A temptation here is to see this practice as merely a technique or strategy. It may be partly that, but I'm encouraging myself (and you by extension) to try to live this way all the time. You might call it a way to respond to the command to "pray without ceasing [and] give thanks in all circumstances" (1 Thess. 5:17-18). Being present in each moment is a practice that requires much practice (see Chapter One), but it also requires God's grace. Giving thanks for God's gift of life is at the heart of living in patience.

A 100-year plan

Elmer and Nadenia Myron, friends of mine and fellow church members back in the 1980s, are members of the Hopi tribe, which settled centuries ago in north central Arizona. Besides being exemplary Mennonites who practice self-sacrifice, service, and humility, they also taught me a lesson about patience. They love their Hopi people and long for them to experience shalom or wholeness. And they are familiar with the injustices Hopis have encountered over the years (along with most Native peoples) from the U.S. government and the wider society. Yet they live with hope. While many of us tend not to think much beyond next week, and others draw up three- or five-year plans, Elmer once told me they think about where they want the Hopi people to be in 100 years. In other words, they look to how what they do now might affect their grandchildren and great-grandchildren, long after they die. How different this is from American short-term thinking!

Most of us who are privileged (I write as a white, American male) are used to having things go our way. (Okay, not always. After all, I root for the Kansas City Royals.) To give our lives working for the betterment of people 100 years from now is difficult to fathom, let alone do. Even (or especially) when our goals are worthy, we are often tempted to look for short-term solutions. A kind of desperation sets in and leads us to belittle those we oppose.

I saw this in the peace movement in the 1980s. As we worked for nuclear disarmament, ending U.S. aid to paramilitary murderers in Central America and aiding refugees from El Salvador, Nicaragua, and Guatemala on their way through the United States to Canada, we often felt discouraged and angry at the Reagan administration, which tended to move in the opposite direction. At every meeting we lapsed into bitter criticism of U.S. policies. We often lacked the discipline to endure and to love our enemies.

Gandhi, King, and many other leaders of nonviolence movements have stressed the importance of discipline, of learning to show respect for those who oppose us. Often we learned most about this discipline from people we were trying to help, people familiar with being oppressed, feeling ground under foot, with no options that seem healthy.

People like the Myrons, like the refugees we hosted, showed me the patience of living day by day, doing what one can, with no certainty that things will get better anytime soon. They were able to bridge that divide between living in reality while hoping for a just future—or what we might call God's kingdom.

How do we get there? How do we learn such patience? One way is through suffering, though that can also lead to bitterness. Another way is the practice of living in the present tense, teaching ourselves to remain alive and attentive in each moment, knowing we are held by God, who is in charge and will somehow bring things around to shalom, that beautiful new Jerusalem.

Chapter Three

Peace

Servanthood replaces dominion. Forgiveness absorbs hostility.
Thus—and only thus—are we bound by New Testament thought to
"be like Jesus."
—John Howard Yoder, *The Politics of Jesus*

More than once, when describing beliefs of Mennonites to a
stranger and mentioning pacifism, I've received this look
that says, "You've got to be kidding." Pacifists are wimps, zany
(or unrealistic, to be nice) and certainly unpatriotic—all traits
that don't sit well with the majority of people in our American
society. Yet we are, alas, pacifists.

In fact, the most distinctive element of Mennonite beliefs
may be its peace position. While interest has grown in other
Christian groups, pacifism is still a minority view. As one of the
Historic Peace Churches (the others being the Church of the
Brethren and the Society of Friends), Mennonites have the
longest history of holding a Christian peace position—now approaching 500 years.

Other groups in other churches have held onto pacifism—
from the Franciscans to the Catholic Worker Movement—as
have many individual Christians. And certainly many other religious groups and individuals have been pacifist, Gandhi being
an outstanding example.

Interestingly, many of these pacifists who are not Christian
point to Jesus as a model. Gandhi referred to Jesus' Sermon on

the Mount (a favorite text of Mennonites) and made the famous comment that Christianity was a great idea that should be tried sometime. While catchy, that quote reflects both the sad state of the church through much of its history and Gandhi's ignorance of church history, which includes much evidence of Christians living like Jesus.

I've referred to the Mennonite "peace position," but many realize there isn't just one. In his book *Nevertheless: Varieties of Religious Pacifism*, well-known Mennonite theologian John Howard Yoder describes at least eighteen kinds of pacifism. I wouldn't claim that Mennonites hold to that many (though if you polled every Mennonite you might find that many or more), but they do adopt several approaches to peace. Two of the chief ones (and I'll say more about this later) are often labeled *nonresistance* and *nonviolent resistance*.

At the same time, some Mennonites—a small minority perhaps—do not hold to a peace position. Some not only support their government going to war but sign up as soldiers. Others may carry or own guns for self-defense. Remember, we're not looking at a monochromatic group. Nevertheless (to borrow Yoder's title) Mennonites are officially a peace church, and some kind of pacifism lies at the heart of Mennonite spirituality.

Peace, you could say, is in our bones.

One of the arguments against pacifism (and many Mennonites accept this) is that it's an add-on to Christian belief, a special discipline or teaching for certain small groups (often called sects). It's nice for these groups to hold onto such quaint, naïve beliefs, but it just wouldn't work if everyone did. The world is a nasty place, the argument goes, and you can't just let people run over you (especially, they may add, if they are enemies of your nation).

In a 2006 profile of Mennonite Church USA members, Conrad L. Kanagy found, for example, that 67 percent of members "would pledge allegiance to the flag," while 48 percent "believe America is a Christian nation." As I said, many Mennonites accept this argument. They believe they are an exception and are glad to let the nation and its soldiers protect them (one of the great myths of our time). This is a crude representation of "nonresistance."

Notice, however, that this argument says nothing about Jesus, nothing about God. The bottom line is that we need to protect ourselves, although that often includes protecting our exorbitant lifestyles. Beneath that belief is the belief that God will not protect us, that our nation, not God, calls the shots.

This leads to the private-public argument: Religion is fine for private morality, but it shouldn't be used to influence public policy. Such a division sounds strange when reading that Jesus proclaimed the good news (gospel) that God rules (Mark 1). God's kingdom is not a private sphere but universal. (I'll say more about this in the next chapter.)

In Mennonite spirituality, peace is not an add-on but an aspect of who God is, who Jesus showed us God is, and who we are to be.

If we believe, as most Christians profess, that Jesus reveals God to us, then peace or nonretaliation is a major aspect of God's nature. And even if we ignore Jesus' teaching and ministry of healing and focus on his passion—his suffering and death on the cross—we still get a strongly nonviolent God.

Altough many Christians focus on the cross as the way Jesus saves us individuals from our individual sins (or sinful nature), the New Testament focuses much more on the social (the public, not the private) meaning of the cross. It brings enemies (Jews and Gentiles, the major division of the world according to the Jews who wrote the New Testament) together, making peace (Eph. 2). Through the cross Jesus "disarmed the rulers and authorities and made a public example of them, triumphing over them in it" (Col. 2:15). Further, "through [Jesus] God was pleased to reconcile to himself all things, whether on earth or in heaven, by making peace through the blood of his cross" (Col. 1:20).

Even in Revelation (not Revelations), misread by many Christians (and others) as a tract for bloodthirsty vengeance, the

Lord is "a lamb standing as if it had been slaughtered" (5:6). The "saints" are told: "If you are to be taken captive, into captivity you go; if you kill with the sword, with the sword you must be killed. Here is a call for endurance and faith of the saints" (13:10). Not exactly a recruiting slogan for the U.S. Army.

Other Christians will raise many objections and quote various verses to try to deny the thrust of the Bible's strong message that God is merciful and that, as Yoder writes, "The cross of Christ is the model of Christian social efficacy, the power of God for those who believe."

An excellent book that addresses the New Testament's message of peace is *Covenant of Peace: The Missing Peace to New Testament Theology and Ethics* by Willard M. Swartley. It's a large volume but worth the effort of reading it for those who, like me, are drawn to study of the Bible.

But hey, I'm a Five in the Enneagram typology, remember? My temptation is knowledge, the need to know, and by that I mean primarily know in my head. Most others operate differently and will not pick up Swartley's book (or Yoder's). They may be more convinced by knowing people who practice peace, which is exactly what Mennonite spirituality calls for.

These ways of knowing can complement one another. For me, a Five, my initial draw to peace was reading—and my own curiosity.

An audacious title

One afternoon in fall 1974, I was in the Better Book Room, a Christian bookstore in Wichita, Kansas. I'd recently begun my last two years of undergraduate study at Wichita State University. On occasion I took a break from studies and work to browse the shelves of this store. That day, a title caught my eye: *The Politics of Jesus*. How audacious! I thought. Jesus had no politics. Curious, I picked it up. The green (almost olive drab) cover included typography of verses from the gospel of Luke's "sermon on the plain" (6:27-36), beginning with, "Be compassionate, as your Father is compassionate." I was familiar with and respected the publisher, Eerdmans, but I knew nothing about the author, one John Howard Yoder, who at that time, said the blurb on the back, was "associate director of the Institute of Mennonite Studies, and President of Goshen Biblical Seminary." I stood there a moment, needing to leave to get to my part-time job. I bought the book.

That evening, I began reading it, and I continued reading it between my studies over the next few weeks. Thereafter my life changed direction.

Maybe it wasn't a drastic change; maybe I would have gone that direction anyway. But looking back, it felt like a crossroad.

After reading that book, I became convinced that pacifism is a true reflection of Jesus' life and teaching. I talked to my Christian friends (seven of us lived together in a house off campus), and several of them read the book. Eventually I became interested in Anabaptist history and theology, in Mennonites, and in intentional community (more on that in the next chapter).

Later I met some Mennonites at a church in Newton, thirty minutes north. They were friendly, hospitable, which was nice, but they were also pacifists, and most hadn't even read Yoder's book. Their church taught about peace but also practiced it, and many of them had been raised in this way from childhood. I was amazed.

War—what is it good for?

Peace is often seen in contrast with war. War is a common expression through history of humanity's worst inclinations: hatred, greed, domination, you name it. It is an evil that destroys not only lives but possibilities. It is a contagion that cannot be healed quickly or easily. It is an addiction that grows as it feeds itself. Killing from one side leads to killing from the other, which leads to . . . a continuous cycle of vengeance.

A favorite tactic of those who belittle pacifism is to claim it isn't realistic, doesn't take evil rulers seriously. These critics ask with upturned noses, So how would you fix this problem (be it Hitler, Stalin, Mao, Pol Pot, Saddam Hussein, the leaders of

Myanmar or Zimbabwe's Mugabe)? War, many think, is a quick solution. Let's invade them or bomb them. Kill the bad guys, and the rest of the people whose country we attacked will flock to our side. Then we act surprised when they hate us even more, and many flock to the side of our enemy. Or we complain when it takes too long to fix this geopolitical problem.

So what would you pacifists do? Well, first of all, acknowledge there are no simple, fast solutions. Also, we'd need to change our mindset, our habits, our expectations. We'd likely have to change the lifestyle we're used to, with the United States consuming a hugely disproportionate share of the world's resources (and China catching up).

We'd also need to work at undoing the enormous damage to relationships that wars have done for centuries: colonialism, for example, or the removal of vast natural resources from various countries without adequate compensation.

Obviously I don't have the expertise to even pretend to have solutions to such problems. Many are working on alternatives to war. Usually these involve such practices as listening to and learning from others, helping those in desperate need, looking for common goals. Such practices have brought more peaceful results than has simple aggression or threats.

Look at the aid given Germany after World War II. One wonders what might have happened if such aid had come after World War I, when Germany was also destitute.

War, as historian Barbara Tuchman has written, is often a "march of folly." It cannot be overcome easily or quickly, but it needs to be overcome. I resonate with the song from the early 1970s that cries, "War—what is it good for? Absolutely nothing."

Since we are not in a position to make such large changes, we do what we can. For Mennonites that has often meant refusing to go to war, refusing to serve in the military. This has meant different approaches in different periods of history. In earlier centuries it meant migration to other countries. This is how many Mennonites ended up in North America. During the

Civil War, many Mennonites paid $300 to avoid being drafted into the army. During World War I, some Mennonites went to prison for refusing to carry a gun in the army. Many of these were beaten and mistreated in other ways. Others (civilians) suffered just for speaking German, others for not buying war bonds or for being pacifists.

World War II brought a change. Mennonite leaders lobbied the U.S. government for alternatives to military service. Out of these talks came Civilian Public Service (CPS). Hundreds of Mennonites and other conscientious objectors served in various camps fighting forest fires, building roads, aiding patients in mental institutions, helping with medical research and in many other ways.

This involvement in CPS had a profound effect on Mennonite involvement in the wider society. Many left agricultural work to become involved in various helping professions, education, business, and other pursuits.

For example, the experience of working in mental institutions, where conditions for patients were often horrific, led Mennonites to begin their own mental health facilities and adopt more humane treatments. (See Chapter Eight.)

What began as a way to avoid the sin of participating in war as soldiers led to more positive involvements that served to build a more peaceful society, not just a pure church.

Mennonites have been debating the goodness and degree of such involvement ever since. Can members work in various professions and work for the betterment of the society without losing their distinctive beliefs and practices? Or, as some have put it, without being stained by the world.

Approaches to peace

This leads to discussions about various approaches to peace. Should Mennonites see the church and world as two kingdoms, one ruled by God and one, for now, by Satan? Should they stay out of trying to change society for the better and focus on being faithful to Jesus (assuming these are mutually exclusive)? Or does God call Mennonites to be agents of change in the world, even to the extent of getting involved in politics? Should they pressure the government to change its policies and make them more in accordance with Christ's ways? Or is such pressure too worldly? Is this mixing the two kingdoms—that of God and that of the world? After all, Jesus said, "My kingdom is not from this world" (John 18:36).

These are serious debates among Mennonites, and I don't see easy answers. I don't see them as either-or. While I believe Mennonites can and should be involved in various professions and seek to be agents of change (of healing and hope, as one Mennonite Church USA statement says), I also believe the temptation to see ourselves rather than God as in charge is great. Practicing Gelassenheit may seem easier when we live more separated from the world (more on that soon), and it may seem harder when confronted with choices about how to exercise power in our work. Either way, we need to develop practices that help keep us aware of who we are and who God is. One key is practicing worship of God as the ruler of all the world, then figuring out with one another's help what our place or vocation is in cooperating with God's work in the world.

Some may feel that God works only (or primarily) in and through the church. But perhaps God works everywhere. Perhaps the Spirit can animate all that we do to help bring greater shalom (more on this word later) to all the world.

Fleeing the world and its ways (however that might be defined) in order not to be conformed to the world has been a strong theme in Mennonite thought, though that language has dissipated lately. Still, there is precedent for this approach throughout Christian history, from the Desert Fathers and Mothers in the third and fourth centuries to the later monastic movements, to the Celts in the wilds of Britain, to the Anabaptists in the sixteenth century, to the many groups who have formed alternative communities right up to the present.

Such a move toward noncomformity can be a mark of humility, recognizing one's weakness, of wisdom, gaining clarity about the Spirit's calling, or of mission, seeing the need for a clear demonstration to the world of what living under God's rule can look like.

This move can also be a mark of fear, of seeking a selfish sense of purity and of naïveté that one can really escape the effects of the world.

All these movements were actually a mixture of separation and involvement, more matters of degree than one or the other. And the best ones—such as the Desert Fathers and Mothers—ended up having a profound influence on the wider church and world, despite the presence of many strange aberrations.

And however one approaches faithfulness in the world, mistakes will occur. A key, most likely, is to act, to seek being faithful and be open to making mistakes and learning from them. Such learning will mean being open to change, something the church—any institution really—has found difficult.

One misunderstanding of peace is that it means only absence of conflict. Certainly it can mean that, and many wish for such peace. And that longing may be behind the push for separation from the world. Get away from the world's conflicts and you find peace, right? We all know the folly of such thinking. All we need do is look at our own families, our own churches.

Yet this thinking is a strong temptation for Mennonites and has led to a perilous habit of conflict avoidance, a pretense that there is no conflict, when in reality the so-called elephant is in the living room.

The sin of "niceness"

I've heard several Mennonites refer to our besetting sin as "niceness." We pretend to be nice while (metaphorically) stabbing each other in the back. Another term for such behavior is being passive-aggressive. I once heard the Methodist theologian Stanley Hauerwas typify his denomination as passive-aggressive. I'd say Methodists don't have a corner on that market.

Mennonites often offer their expertise in conciliation, helping other groups work through conflict and arrive at some peaceful agreement. Yet among ourselves we often act abysmally toward each other—making decisions that affect others' lives without even talking to them first, talking to others about someone without first talking to the person with whom we disagree.

A friend of mine was applying for a position with Mennonite Church USA and waited for days after the deadline by which she had been promised a decision. She tried contacting the person making the decision but could not reach her. Then on a Friday, after my friend had gone home from work, the human resources person left a message on her answering machine that she did not get the job.

We don't like to face each other and talk over our conflicts. We'd rather help others do that.

Another example revolves around the issue of homosexuality. (Calling that the issue is itself an oversimplification and a way of avoidance.) Over many years, the Mennonite magazine I worked for included occasional articles on this topic. Invariably we received many letters from readers either denouncing those who accept "homosexuals" in the church or denouncing those who do not accept such people. Actually the church's official position is that we accept people with a homosexual orientation but not if they "practice" it. (And you can debate just what that means.)

In print, it seemed, people felt free to express their strong opinions, pro or con. Meanwhile, I saw little conciliation happening. It appeared to be people on two extremes yelling (via the page) at each other, while the people in the middle who weren't sure what they believed or who saw no clear solutions were left out. At the same time—and this is my point—people weren't talking to each other face-to-face. Print was a handy way to avoid such contact.

What makes this behavior ironic and sad is that the early Anabaptists emphasized what they called "the rule of Christ," which derives from Matthew 18:15: "If another member of the church sins against you, go and point out the fault when the two of you are alone." The following verses (16-20) go on to outline a practice of reaching agreement over contentious issues. This rule formed the basis for Anabaptist community (see the next chapter).

In my experience, this practice is hard yet leads to harmony and growth. About every time I go to persons to point out how they have sinned against me, I learn that I also have sinned against them. Eventually, sometimes with pastoral help from others, we reach a point of mutual confession and forgiveness. But each time someone does something that bugs me, I need to look at why it bugs me and not simply blame the other person.

Many of us practice this kind of peacemaking in our families and with our spouses. I'll never forget the older woman who said to me in the reception line at my wedding, "The best advice for a good marriage is to say, 'I'm sorry.'" Whenever Jeanne or I talk about something the other has done that we don't like, we usually each end up saying, "I'm sorry."

Can we extend such practice to our relationships in the church? Mennonite spirituality says that "peace" includes making right our relationships with each other. And I would emphasize "making" as much as "right" in that sentence. We not only want to arrive at peace in our relationships, we want to work toward such peace in a peaceful way. As the Fellowship of Reconciliation says, "Peace is the way to peace."

The meaning of shalom

Peace is all-encompassing. The Hebrew word usually translated "peace" is *shalom*. In his book *Shalom: The Bible's Word for Salvation, Justice and Peace*, Mennonite Old Testament scholar Perry Yoder writes that "shalom . . . has three shades of meaning." These can be summarized as material well-being, justice and straightforwardness. He writes,

> This means that shalom in the Bible involves a much wider and more positive state of affairs than a narrow understanding of peace as antiwar or antimilitary activity. Shalom making is working for just and health-giving relationships between people and nations.

"Shalom defines how things should be," writes Yoder, and thus represents God's ultimate will. The tension of the real and the ideal, what is and what ought to be, is reflected in the pursuit of shalom—how things ought to be.

And shalom, God's ultimate will, applies to all creation— the plant and animal world as well as the relationships of human beings. Many who hear that Mennonites believe in peace—including many Mennonites—immediately think in political terms. They're against war. Or they won't join the army.

But the heart of Mennonite spirituality beats in tune with a desire in God's heart that the creation God called "very good" (Gen. 1:31) will experience healing in all its facets. That includes healing the conflicts between nations and between neighbors, healing the warring, destructive desires in our souls, healing the wounded earth and poisoned waters and scarred sky.

The apostle Paul writes that "the whole creation has been groaning in labor pains" (Rom. 8:22). We too "groan inwardly" (8:23). God's creation, including us, is good but needs the Spirit's healing touch. By pursuing shalom (Psalm 34:14) we cooperate with God's work in the world. Such pursuit takes many forms.

Using shalom instead of peace helps us get past the misunderstanding that peace is primarily theoretical, nonmaterial, an amorphous feeling. Shalom is inherently physical; it concerns our material well-being—and not merely ours. Experiencing shalom does not mean we load up on food or pleasures but that everyone has what they need.

Gnostic behavior

Much of Christianity has adopted a Gnostic attitude toward the body. The early church engaged in arguments with Gnostic beliefs that the body is evil, "a prison house for the soul." In some Gnostic writings, the God of the Old Testament who created the world was really an evil being who sought to imprison souls in the physical world. True knowledge ("gnosis") could free believers from this physical world, the prison, to experience salvation.

While Christians today don't use this kind of language and would not call the Creator evil, many act as if salvation or peace has little or nothing to do with the body, our physical presence. Salvation is an escape from this fallen world to heaven. Thus any actions that help people's physical needs or help the environment are either means for what really matters (we feed the hungry to preach the gospel to them) or are at best secondary to what's truly important or are irrelevant.

Such Gnostic behavior denies the incarnation, that in Jesus God "became flesh and lived among us" (John 1:14). And while Christians profess belief in the incarnation, many are not comfortable with its implications.

They will say that the peace that matters is peace with God, which means that an angry God has been placated by Jesus' death, and we can get into heaven. Other kinds of peace are nice but not necessary.

Shalom is something different. You can't read the Bible long without at least noticing—despite our inbred denial—how concerned it is with our material lives. All those detailed guidelines for worship and daily living that sound so foreign to us are nevertheless addressing day-to-day, physical situations. And the Psalms often call upon God for salvation from enemies—real, physical enemies. In his translation of the Psalms, Robert Alter often uses the word *rescue* instead of "save," emphasizing that the Psalmist is being rescued from physical danger, not just (or even) going to heaven.

Then there's the Letter of James, which Luther called a "gospel of straw" and wanted to remove form the canon. James defines religion as caring "for orphans and widows in their distress, and [keeping] oneself unstained by the world" (1:27). He goes on to ask what good it is to say to someone in need, "Go in peace; keep warm and eat your fill," yet not supply their bodily needs (2:16).

Luther and others worry that such statements will lead to "works righteousness," trying to win favor from God by our own works.

From its beginnings, Mennonite spirituality has emphasized faith and practice as inseparable (see Chapter One). God's grace not only forgives us but empowers us through the Holy Spirit to live out shalom, what God wants for all the creation. We don't help orphans and widows or feed the hungry out of fear of what God might do to us. We do it out of love for God and for our neighbor, as Jesus showed us.

We honor God's creation in treating all of life with respect and love. That is practicing shalom, which means helping bring material well-being—justice—to all. And "all" includes the world ("kosmos") that God so loved (John 3:16).

Being peace

Peace, or shalom, has many dimensions, including our own temperament or mindset. The Buddhist monk Thich Nhat Hanh writes about "being peace." He teaches that experiencing peace through meditation helps us effect peace in the world. Meditating for our own peaceful state is not true peace. Neither is working frantically for peace in the world while we express anger and hatred. We should seek to become a peace presence in the world, he writes.

Thich Nhat Hanh is no naïve dreamer, however. He has faced suffering and been exiled from his native Vietnam for his work for peace. Being peace requires difficult practice in a community that also seeks to pursue shalom.

I've been tempted by both directions—finding individual peace of mind and actively working for peace in the world while exhibiting much unpeaceful behavior.

In the 1980s, when I was more actively involved in the peace movement, particularly in seeking nuclear disarmament, I often felt such anger toward the U.S. government and corporations such as McDonnell-Douglass, General Electric, and others, which poured millions of dollars into armaments—not only for the already burgeoning U.S. arsenal but for warring factions overseas—including landmines that maimed many children. I tried to find peace within, but that felt hollow and selfish. I realized I had—and continue to have—much to learn about being peace.

Experiencing peace oneself and sharing that peace with others by our presence is a great challenge. And trying to do it alone is not only unwise but unbiblical. (More on this in the next chapter.)

Simple practices can help us. Thich Nhat Hanh describes how a smile can have a wonderful effect on others as well as ourselves. Try it. Smile and note the effect it has on your attitude and your body. Then experiment with others. Smile (appropriately, of course) and note how it affects them.

Thich Nhat Hanh offers a short guide to breathing and smiling:

Breathing in, I calm my body.
Breathing out, I smile.
Dwelling in the present moment
I know this is a wonderful moment. (*Being Peace*)

Nonanxious presence

People who work in conciliation talk about the importance of the mediator exhibiting a nonanxious presence (see Chapter Eight). As the two sides, each anxious to promote its point of view and oppose the other's, state their positions, the mediator must calmly help each side understand and state the other's viewpoint. That calm is an important element in the mediation and has a calming effect on the parties.

Whether or not we are involved in mediation, formally or otherwise, we, too, can have a calming, peaceful effect on others as we demonstrate nonanxious presence in each part of our daily lives. Doing so requires much practice and encouragement from others.

You may have noticed how the various aspects of a Mennonite spirituality, which I've delineated by chapters, are interrelated. And I've emphasized their connection by beginning each chapter title with the letter *P*. I've also made repeated references to later or earlier chapters that relate to the point I'm making.

Thus, for example, we need patience to practice peace. Peace helps us practice patience, which is an element of peace. And both patience and peace are mere theoretical constructs until we put them into practice. And soon we will see that we cannot do any of this on our own but must do it in the context of politics, in a decision-making community.

Chapter Four

Politics

Christianity means community through Jesus Christ and in Jesus Christ.
—Dietrich Bonhoeffer, *Life Together*

After Christ it is no longer possible to separate the love of God from the love of the brothers and sisters.
—Carlo Carretto

Each of us looks at the world through a specific set of lenses. We approach situations and other people from a certain perspective. We read the Bible from a viewpoint shaped by a complex array of experiences—including ways we've been taught to read it, the fortunes or misfortunes we've had, the people we've encountered who have helped us and hurt us, the places we've lived, our society and our place in it, our gender or class or race or other sociological constructs, and on and on.

I'm not saying our lives are determined either genetically or by our environment, and I'm not qualified to delineate how much freedom we possess. I am saying that we do not come to our view of the world or our faith from a blank slate, which most people would acknowledge. Neither am I saying that all truth is relative. I'm saying we come to our faith searching, not certain. As John D. Caputo writes, "Faith is idolatrous if it is rigidly self-certain but not if it is softened in the waters of 'doubt'" (*What Would Jesus Deconstruct?*).

Remember my emphasis in the preface on the smallest word in my title (or subtitle): *A*. I use that word to communicate not the importance of my opinion or point of view but the reality that what you're reading is one perspective. And you, with the lenses you've formed in your life, can read this and respond however you deem best.

In acknowledging that each of us in our context brings a different perspective, I'm also noting that a key part of that context—twenty-first century North America, say—is the view that the individual is pre-eminent. We tend to see ourselves primarily as autonomous individuals and resist the notion that we are (we might add "merely") part of a group. We like to think of ourselves as unique, not quite like anyone else.

While that is true, it is also true that in many ways we are not unique, and our consumeristic culture reinforces that. More and more, we buy our food and clothes at similar stores, watch similar programs on TV, and respond to events in similar ways. Marketing forces try to induce feelings of uniqueness to a mass audience. And they succeed by both knowing and fooling their audience. You could say we often conform to images of non-comformity.

Few of us realize how different people's perspectives were in earlier centuries. Those living in biblical times, even in the first century A.D., would likely find our notion of the autonomous individual completely foreign. They did not identify themselves as individuals but as members of a family or clan, a tribe, a people. (Jesus was Jesus bar-Joseph, or son of Joseph.) And by family I don't mean what we call the nuclear family (parents and children) but parents, children, grandparents, servants (depending on the family's wealth), and any other relatives that fit into the domicile. Rodney Clapp writes that many Christians today "exalt a 'traditional family' that is hardly two centuries old, a kind of family decisively shaped by the advent of capitalism and industrialization" (*Border Crossings*).

So when we read about the Philippian jailer believing in Jesus and being baptized (Acts 16:25-34), the phrase "you and your household" gives us pause. Did not each person need to make up his or her own mind and believe and be baptized individually? And wouldn't at least one not follow suit? Why even use such a phrase?

Old Testament scholars have noted the idea of a corporate identity in the Bible. The New Testament promotes the notion that Jesus Christ is "the head of the body, the church" (Col. 1:18) and that "there is one body and one Spirit" (Eph. 4:4).

And while today there are thousands of Christian denominations, Ephesians 4:3 calls believers not to manufacture unity but to "maintain the unity of the Spirit." The unity is there to be lived out.

If we read such language honestly, we'll likely acknowledge its strangeness to our understanding. It must mean some ethereal unity on another plane. Yet the Bible is concrete in its thought, even visceral. It calls believers not just to think their faith but live it out in real life. Thus unity, being one body, is to be a concrete reality.

The church as family

From its beginnings, Mennonite spirituality has emphasized community, the harmony of believers, of those called brothers and sisters. This idea of the church as a family comes from Jesus, who said to a crowd at one point, "Who are my mother and my brothers?" Then he answered his rhetorical question, "Here are my brother and sister and mother" (Mark 3:33-35).

Adopting the notion that our faith community is our primary family is countercultural, to be kind, or heretical, to be less kind. Only cults would demand such misguided loyalty, right?

But this begs the question, What do we do with what Jesus said? It's interesting to note that just before that statement in Mark's Gospel, the text says that Jesus' family "went out to restrain him, for people were saying, 'He has gone out of his mind'" (Mark 3:21). Jesus, too, it seems, was deemed heretical, even crazy.

I have sympathy both for those being labeled heretical and those concerned about groups having too much control over their members. Let me explain.

During my last two semesters in college (at Wichita State) I became interested in intentional community. The book *Living Together in a World Falling Apart,* by Dave and Neta Jackson, led me to visit Reba Place Fellowship in Evanston, Illinois, where the Jacksons were members. Reba Place was at the time one of the oldest of the growing number of intentional Christian communities. Many of these communities, like Reba Place, required their members to pool their resources in a common treasury. Thus a person or family who joined would turn over their assets and liabilities to the community, which then owned those monies and property.

The inspiration for such an arrangement was the early church in Jerusalem as recorded in Acts 2:44-45 and 4:32-37. Other passages in the New Testament imply that similar communities existed elsewhere. (See Reta Finger's *Of Widows and Meals.*) For example, 2 Thessalonians 3:10 says, "Anyone unwilling to work should not eat," which implies that work and eating were common activities and that a community had some say in who did what.

I took a train to Chicago over Christmas break in 1975 and spent almost a week at Reba Place. I loved the life I found there—the warm hospitality, the vitality of worship, the many ways people (both members and neighbors) were being helped.

Another appeal to me of this arrangement was that it helped one respond to Jesus' admonition to the rich young ruler (Mark just calls him "a man" but adds that "he had many possessions"): "Go, sell what you own, and give the money to the poor, . . . then come, follow me" (Mark 10:21).

When I told my housemates (seven of us lived together in a house off campus), they said they were happy I had found what I wanted but sad to have me move so far away.

When I told my parents, they were not happy—either to have me move so far away or because of the arrangement, which went against some of their basic beliefs, such as the belief in capitalism that most Americans share. I did not tell them how certain I was that I wanted to join Reba Place, only that I was interested. This allowed them to hold out hope that I would change my mind eventually, once I came to my senses.

As the end of the spring semester (and graduation) approached, I remained interested in moving to Reba Place, but I also felt some misgivings about moving so far. Despite the fact that I had attended four different colleges, I remained one who preferred routines, the knowable. Uncertainty, such as about what life at Reba Place would be like for me as a member, left me nervous.

Then one afternoon in May 1976, only a week or two before finals, I received a call from Peggy Belser, my contact at Reba Place. She said the leaders of the fellowship thought it best for me to live closer to my parents. They recommended I go to New Creation Fellowship (NCF), one of their sister communities, in Newton, just thirty minutes north of Wichita. I'd visited there a few times, and the people there were friendly, but it was so small, only fifteen or so adult members, while Reba Place had more than 100.

I asked her if this was a requirement. She said no; it was my decision to make, but this is what they felt was best.

I hung up the phone feeling rejected, my dream crushed. When I shared the news with my two closest friends in the house, they tried to be sympathetic but couldn't hide their pleasure that I might not move so far away.

After a period (days, a week) of thinking and praying about what I should do, I realized that both my desire to be in a bigger and more exciting place and my questioning of what the community thought best went against the spirit of community I wanted to be part of. (I almost wrote "make a part of my life," then realized that betrays the individualistic consumerism community opposes.) I became more comfortable with the idea of moving just a ways north, bringing me even closer geographically to my parents in Emporia.

I visited NCF again and told someone there (Steve Schmidt, I believe) about my conversation with Peggy. He said I'd be welcome to make an extended visit and "discern with them" (a favorite phrase of these communities) if I should join them.

Soon I decided not to go to Reba Place but to NCF. I told my parents, and they were happy. They had resigned themselves to the notion that I was going to join a community, so my decision to go to one closer to home was a kind of victory.

I stayed in Wichita that summer doing yard work and then traveled with two friends in late July to Regent College in Vancouver, British Columbia, where we each took a three-week course. I took New Testament Social Ethics, taught by John Howard Yoder, whose books had influenced me so much.

The move to NCF

Finally, in late August, I moved into a room on the third floor of a three-story house on West Eleventh Street in Newton. NCF owned five houses in a two-block area. The "corner house," where I lived, and the "free house" (given to NCF by a group of doctors, though it had to be moved across town) next door formed one of two "extended households." Ours, named Alabaré ("I will praise" in Spanish, also the name of a song we sang in worship), consisted of three married couples, five children (ages one to seven), and two single men (soon joined by a single woman attending a local college). Down the block was Walkway, named for the path that joined the two houses that made up that household. It consisted of two couples, four children (ages four to nine), and three single women. At the fifth house lived a couple with two children.

Allowing me to move into a household before joining the fellowship was an exception to the usual practice up to that time. However, I'd assured Steve, Alabaré's head of household and one of NCF's two elders (or pastors), that I was set on joining, which meant turning over all my assets and liabilities and committing myself to NCF "for life, or until the Lord called me elsewhere," as was the understanding. And being called elsewhere, I knew, would need to be discerned by the community. Such a commitment was not to be taken lightly, Steve told me, and they liked to give people time to visit and understand what it means before joining.

I joined on October 10, less than two months after moving in. They used a Sunday morning worship (held in the basement of the free house) as the setting for the ceremony celebrating my joining. It didn't feel difficult at all; this is what I'd wanted for some time. The economic part, so hard for my parents to accept, was easy for me. I had few assets and no liabilities, no college debts. The car I'd been using during college belonged to my parents, and I returned it to them.

I felt completely happy. Sometimes I felt like pinching myself because this was what I'd dreamed of. I couldn't believe I was finally here.

My parents, however, were not so happy with this arrangement. They didn't say much, but I knew they had their suspicions. Once I made a comment to my mother about cults like the Moonies (the Unification Church). She said, "How is your group different?"

That she had that question startled me.

NCF's approach to family members and others who had questions about us was to invite them to "come and see," as Jesus told two of John the Baptist's disciples (John 1:39). This worked well, partly because it was difficult to explain such a life together and mostly because the people at NCF were friendly and non-defensive (for the most part). My parents visited several times, and while they continued to disagree with the financial arrangement, they liked the people there. The fellowship grew in numbers as people visited the worship services, then hung around, became part of a small group, then eventually joined. Soon we created a third household and called a new elder to lead that.

"Calling an elder" introduces the question of how that happened, which introduces the topic of decision-making, which is a key element of politics, the title of this chapter. So let's address this briefly.

Making decisions together

"Politics" derives from the Greek work *polis*, often translated "city" but primarily denoting a decision-making body. Besides starting with P, politics reflects the workings of a community of people making decisions together to carry out their goals, the kind of life they've set for themselves. That dynamic is one more key element of Mennonite spirituality.

While "politics" carries a complex of meanings related to governing or setting policy, it also has for many a pejorative sense ("Oh, that's just politics") that identifies it with seeking power at the expense of truth or justice. The politics of Jesus, which Yoder used as the title for his groundbreaking book, is one of servanthood, not dominance. This kind of decision-making out of a unity in the Spirit, within which no one person dominates, is what the church is called to practice.

The Greek word usually translated "church" in the New Testament is *ekklesia*, which describes a smaller decision-making body, often like what we'd call a town meeting.

The passage (Matt. 18:15-20) that includes what the early Anabaptist movement called "the rule of Christ," which we looked at earlier, is about decision-making, about discernment, about figuring out who's telling the truth in a conflict and what is the right course of action. It includes two references to "the church" and concludes with the familiar sentence, "For where two or three are gathered in my name, I am there among them" (v. 20).

In Mennonite spirituality, community discernment is a big deal. It's how we are to read the Bible. We study it individually, but we are to talk about what it means with our brothers and sisters. It also emphasizes the participation of everyone. Mennonites tend to resist decrees from on high. They even object to there being an "on high." And while most Mennonite churches vote on candidates for pastor and other matters, such as the church budget, some, like NCF, operate on a consensus model in which everyone must agree on a course of action before it goes forward.

So when the two NCF elders recommended that Lynn Loucks be a third elder, the decision was made by all the members, and for it to go forward we had to either agree or abstain from the decision. If we opposed it, it didn't go forward. We waited, kept talking, or tried something else.

This doesn't discount the influence those elders had, but their recommendation was not a guarantee. I saw decisions stopped by one person saying no.

And when you're set up as a common treasury, in which all monies and property are held in common, many decisions need to be made. Economics, we learned, affects just about everything. The private-public split usually used to make religion a private affair all but disappears.

It's about economics

The Bible addresses economics throughout its pages. The "Torah" (usually translated "Law") was a way of life that was to help Israel, the community of God's people, live in harmony (shalom). Sabbath and Jubilee laws helped ensure that everyone had enough and that no one had a disproportionate amount of resources. One sign of a just society, according to the Bible, was how it cared for the most vulnerable, "widows and orphans," who had no one else to care for them. And Jesus, many have pointed out, spoke more about money ("mammon") than any other topic. Look at the story of Zacchaeus (Luke 19:1-10). When the little man says to Jesus he will give half his possessions to the poor and pay back four times as much anyone he has defrauded, Jesus says, "Today salvation has come to this house."

When economic sharing is at the core of a community's identity, then all aspects of its life are affected. One telling example is that when a couple at NCF wanted to have a baby, that was a community decision, for, to put it crassly, we were all paying for that baby. Also we all were going to help raise it and love it (ahem, him or her). I should add that such a decision was handled sensitively, to the best of my knowledge. Many other decisions were not as easy, however, and required much time and much agonizing. One thing that made it hard was that people had different priorities, and we came to NCF from different situations and with different perspectives.

Looking back, I think we erred in not being more flexible and giving families more discretion in how they spent for their needs. For example, one couple might sacrifice certain things to visit family members that lived far away. Another couple might sacrifice other things to pursue some alternative ways to address health problems.

Another thing that affected this was how much money we had coming in. We usually had just enough—never a lot. But by pooling income we were able to commit several leaders to various ministries. For example, a woman with five young children came to us, fleeing an abusive husband. She and her children moved into our household and lived there for more than a year. The mother helped with cooking, cleaning, and childcare but also needed some counseling and other emotional support. She brought in no income, but enough people did to allow her to stay. One elder spoke often with her husband, and while they did not reconcile, they reached a certain level of peace. Eventually she and her children moved to California and were doing well, the last I heard.

The kind of decision-making (often regarding finances) NCF did was similar to what a family would do. But in a larger community such politics, as it were, are much more complicated. A large part of the vision or goal of communities like NCF was to be such a community. While ministry happened and a high level of efficiency was reached because of how we were set up, that wasn't the primary reason for it. The vision was to be an alternative community that demonstrated what living under God's rule might look like. Even more basic was our desire to love God and each other.

The experience of being part of an intentional community (the common treasury ended at the end of 1985, following a long and crippling audit by the IRS) left many lasting impressions on me and convinced me that being part of a church community, in whatever form it takes, is of central importance in being a faithful follower of Jesus.

Love is a gift

One impression—perhaps the most important—I received was being known and loved by others. A central belief at NCF was that God loves us unconditionally. In other words, love is a gift, not something earned. I remember hearing the message, Nothing I do can make God love me more or less. I can neither impress God with my good deeds nor drive God away with my bad deeds.

Such a truth is humbling but also difficult to believe if it is merely theoretical. What made it more possible for me to believe was that others at NCF—my brothers and sisters— demonstrated that unconditional love to me.

As happens in families, the other members get to know you pretty well when you're rubbing shoulders and grating egos every day. Living in a household with others makes it difficult to carry out the pretense that you've got your act together. Soon the junk in your life gets exposed. Often it's the so-called little things that get to you. I never had a theological argument with others in my household. (No one else seemed all that interested in theology.) But we argued about how we squeezed the common toothpaste tube or who neglected to do their chores or what kind of music someone listened to in the common area and when.

I disliked being around one man about my age. We were in the same household and worked together on the NCF Builders, a remodeling crew. As you know by now, I'm introverted and prefer reading to talking at length with people, especially people who only want to talk about themselves. This man liked to talk at length about himself.

I tried to pretend to be a good Christian who listened attentively to others, but I couldn't pull that off for long. Soon this man employed the rule of Christ and confronted me. He had insight, and despite my efforts I had to admit I'd been looking down on him as a needy person while I had my act together. But in fact my act was falling apart. I was as needy as he was, but he was mature enough to admit his need.

In our household meetings we often talked about conflicts and how we were doing. I remember my shock one of the first times I shared a shortcoming of mine. No one seemed surprised that I had shortcomings. They demonstrated two things: (1) they accepted my failures and forgave me when I did something wrong; (2) they weren't as impressed as I thought they should be with what a great Christian I was. In those two ways they showed unconditional love and thus reflected God's love to me.

The effect on me was palpable. I relaxed more. I realized I'd been carrying a weight of anxiety and tension, either trying to live up to a standard I'd set or worrying about being rejected for screwing up. The lessened anxiety did not come overnight and was not necessarily dramatic, but I noticed it. You could call it the freedom of humility. When you don't worry about impressing others or messing up around them, you are freer.

Community is a good place to learn that the world does not revolve around you, something the marketing forces want us to believe. A saying was going around NCF back then that I even printed on a T-shirt (by hand): "It's important, but it really doesn't matter." That paradox (maybe it's a straight contradiction) acknowledged that certain things were important but then put them in perspective. Ultimately they're not that important.

It reminds me of what Paul wrote to the Roman Christians who were judging one another for their practices regarding food sacrificed to idols: "The kingdom of God is not food and drink but righteousness and peace and joy in the Holy Spirit" (Rom. 14:17). He calls upon his readers (listeners really) to "pursue what makes for peace and for mutual upbuilding" (14:19) and concludes with the admonition that sums up how to live in Christian community: "Welcome one another . . . just as Christ has welcomed you, for the glory of God" (15:7).

As people at NCF loved me unconditionally, I grew more able to do the same. And that included my parents, strangely enough. As others loved me unconditionally, I realized I didn't feel that kind of love from my father. And consequently I was carrying hurts and resentments from and toward him. Eventually, after much struggle, I was able to forgive him—in my heart, as it were.

Amazingly to me, things changed. The little habits he had that had always bothered me no longer did. (I realized I was like him in many ways, which probably contributed to my irritation.) I felt more relaxed around him, not needing him to treat me a certain way. We became more like peers and got along well when we were together. I got interested in researching our ancestors, and in 1986 we took a trip together back east to look through some historical records and the places where my great-grandparents (his grandparents) lived. I told him regularly that I loved him. And when he died, in 1997, I felt at peace with him.

During this time my parents became more accepting of my life at NCF. That increased when they met Jeanne, a member of NCF before I came, whom I married in 1979. This seemed to prove to them that I could make at least one good decision.

I understand better the tensions of family loyalty versus commitment to a church family and how these are accentuated when the commitment to a church community is rigorous. Such a commitment goes against the American way of life and can seem weird, if not crazy. Yet peace can also come in this tension. Apparently Jesus' mother was with him at the cross, and his brothers (or cousins, if you believe Mary remained a virgin) became followers.

Figuring out what God wants and doing it

In earlier chapters I've written about some implications of believing that God—not America or Madison Avenue or my own ego—rules. Our task—one of them anyway—as Christians is to try to figure out what God wants. Then we are to do that as best we can.

Mennonite spirituality teaches that both these tasks—figuring out what God wants and doing it—are made easier, even made possible, by being in a community of people also committed to following God's rule.

One way this is practiced is in interpreting Scripture, which is one of our chief guides in figuring out what God wants. In the sixteenth century, the early Anabaptists opposed the notion that only the Roman Catholic Church hierarchy could interpret Scripture. They also opposed the teaching of the Protestant Reformers that the individual was the main mediator of Scripture. Instead they taught that Christ was present in the gathered body and that the Spirit led that body in interpreting the Scriptures. And the goal of interpretation was not merely to understand but to obey God's Word to them. And the community was there not only to interpret but to help one another obey what they understood.

Although we tend to dislike the term, this is politics—deciding together how to live our lives. As with any human community, mistakes and excesses occur. One practice of community discipline among early Anabaptists was shunning. This practice was intended to help a straying member return to the fold.

Most Mennonites today don't practice this, or if they do, it's done more subtly (see passive aggression). This is so partly in reaction to excesses in the past (there's the story, probably apocryphal, of a minister in Holland long ago who shunned everyone in the church except his wife) and partly (mostly perhaps) due to the influence of individualism. We've come to accept that most people make up their own minds. Also, belonging to a certain church is not that big a deal, if one doesn't demand that kind of obedience.

For example, I know a man who belonged to a certain Mennonite church, but during World War II he joined the Navy. His church excommunicated him, and when he got out of the Navy, he joined a different Mennonite church.

Again, I sympathize with both parties here. One was holding to a standard of behavior (not joining the military), the other to a standard of welcoming those who wish to join. Here is another tension in Mennonite spirituality: How do we call one another to obedience to Jesus' teaching and also welcome one another as Christ welcomes us?

This, you see, is a political dilemma. Each community has to decide together how to respond to situations that arise. Often such decisions are not easy, and we find our way by trial and error.

NCF began in 1973 as an intentional community in which members pooled their resources into a common treasury. I joined in 1976. Several years later, a member questioned this requirement for membership. He contended that persons should be able to join a church on the basis of their confession of faith in Jesus Christ. We discussed it, argued about it, sought counsel from other church leaders, even some biblical scholars we knew. Throughout its short history, NCF had had many people participate in its worship services without becoming members. This often felt awkward, but many of us members felt that such a commitment was necessary to carry out the intense life we wanted to pursue.

We faced that common dilemma: whether to be welcoming or to call for following Jesus in a concrete way. How could we do both?

Eventually we decided to allow people to join the church without having to join the common treasury. It seemed right, and I'll always admire the man who pushed for this, even though he and I argued often. He was a member and didn't threaten to leave. He argued persistently but not angrily. He showed us respect, even though he thought we were wrong.

After we changed membership requirements, people began leaving the common treasury, and few if any joined. This coincided with a harsh IRS audit (Kafkaesque in its punitive catch-22s) that forced us to sell houses to pay taxes they ruled we owed, plus twenty percent interest. The same thing was happening to some of our sister communities as well as to other Christian communities across the country. After five years or so, the common treasury, with only eight of us left as members, dissolved.

This painful yet necessary step was one more event in the life of a Mennonite congregation trying to live as faithful followers of Jesus Christ. NCF continues today, having gone through various changes, as have all churches. Jeanne and I continue as members, and the dilemma of how to be faithful and welcoming continues, though in different ways.

Intimate and open

A particular dilemma in many Mennonite congregations, where community is a high value, is how to maintain an intimate community while being open to newcomers.

I've heard people say about our congregation and others that the people there seem to know each other well, like a family, but that visitors feel like unwelcome outsiders who have difficulty breaking into the circle. It can feel like coming to church and discovering you're at a family reunion.

The long ethnic identity of many Mennonites in North America has contributed to this problem. Coming to these shores as a persecuted minority, many Mennonites kept to themselves in their own communities, mostly rural, and their children married the children of other Mennonites. In time, most Mennonites in North America had one of a few dozen German or Swiss names, such as Yoder, Miller, Schmidt, Epp, Roth, Hershberger, Dyck, Janzen, Penner, Preheim, Schrag, Kauffman (or Kaufman or Kauffmann), Klassen (or Classen or Claassen), and others.

When one Mennonite met another and heard his or her name, he or she might ask, Are you related to so-and-so? While people who first meet often look for common interests or experiences, they don't usually look for common relatives. Many Mennonites, however, do. This is called the Mennonite Game. Many people see it as an insidious practice that leaves people without those so-called Mennonite names feeling excluded. I often saw it as a curiosity. When I began working for a Mennonite denomination in 1978, I met other Mennonites and introduced myself. When they heard my name, Houser, a quizzical look often came to their face. I soon added, "I didn't grow up Mennonite." They'd smile as if forgiving me this short-coming and welcome me into the fold. Perhaps I should have felt offended, since I'd already been a member of a Mennonite congregation for a few years, but I just smiled back.

Part of the curiosity is that this behavior, this game, goes against Mennonite theology, which teaches that one becomes a Mennonite by choice, being baptized upon confession of faith in Christ.

People who claimed Mennonite as an ethnic identity used to rile me up. (Now it mildly irritates me.) I once wrote an edi-torial called "Mennonite Christian is Redundant," in which I said that "Mennonite" is—or should be—a marker of faith, not ethnicity.

My mother-in-law, who was Catholic, grew up with many of the same ethnic markers that others call Mennonite. Her an-cestors were German-speaking Catholics in Russia who came to America to avoid conscription. She picked up some Low Ger-man growing up and ate some of the same dishes Mennonites ate. In the editorial I wrote, "I didn't join the Mennonite church because it ate borscht."

I received a letter in response to the editorial from a woman in Canada, where "Mennonite" is more commonly seen as an ethnic marker. She claimed to be proud to be a Mennonite, but she did not believe in God. That, to me, was a contradiction.

A growing number of writers in Canada are labeled Men-nonite because they grew up in a Mennonite family, even though they are not part of Mennonite churches. I don't like such confusion, but I suppose it's a losing battle to oppose it. On a much larger scale, many "Jewish" writers in the United States are not practicing Jews.

To be clear, while I recognize this ethnic identity phenome-non, I use the term *Mennonite* as a faith identity. Since the ma-jority of Mennonites in the world do not have German or Swiss names (many have Hispanic or Congolese names, for example), it's ridiculous to make such an identification. Yet I believe such behavior betrays our hunger for connection. God has made us communal beings, part of one humanity, part of God's creation. In many and various ways we act out our longing for connection with others. Looking for common names or practices is one more way to seek such connection.

Mennonites have developed strong communal ties. This is a good trait and arises from a theology of communal unity, discipline, and decision-making. Our challenge is to make our communities more permeable. Another word for this is hospitality.

While God gave Israel the Torah (Law) to learn to live in healthy ways as a faithful community, that Torah included commands to welcome the stranger (alien, foreigner) in their midst.

One direction we might look to learn hospitality is the emergent church, particularly in relating to spiritual seekers from a postmodern context. Instead of following the usual order of including newcomers—they believe, then learn to behave before they belong—the emergent church helps people belong, then learn behavior, which then helps them believe.

I see this tension between community and hospitality in the New Testament. At the Last Supper, possibly a seder meal, the disciples are with Jesus, relatively safe. Seven weeks later comes Pentecost, where the Spirit falls upon a diverse crowd, and a torrent of outreach ensues. A close community of followers committed to Jesus' difficult way becomes a movement that spreads throughout the ancient world, welcoming people from many tribes and tongues. The early Anabaptist movement, which began among three men in a room, also spread across Europe.

The temptation of community is to make it comfortable and safe. It then becomes static, and we do not grow in our life in God. Healthy community will lead us through tensions and welcome people into our midst. And as we learned in those early years at NCF (and continue to learn), each new person who joins us changes us. This is the dynamic life of the Spirit, helping make us agents of healing and hope in the world.

Jeremy Begbie uses music as an analogy for this need to welcome change:

Music . . . teaches us how not to rush over tension, how to find joy and fulfillment through a temporal movement that includes struggles, clashes, and fractures. The temptation is to pass over what needs to be passed through. (*Resounding Truth: Christian Wisdom in the World of Music*)

Communists

One of the tensions we experienced when NCF was a common treasury was between that practice and the surrounding capitalistic culture. That none of us owned cars or houses was considered strange not just to my parents but to most people we encountered, including other Mennonites. The Cold War was still on, and a few called us communists, and I suppose we were, but our motivation was to follow Jesus and practice love toward one another.

We were not trying to uphold an economic practice on our own steam or convert society to communism. We all grew up in a capitalistic culture, and holding things in common was not easy. While technically we owned nothing, we each had clothes we wore (though we did some trading), books and records we brought when we joined (though many of these were put in a common living room), and each month we got an allowance of $30 for personal use. Our guideline for that was Mennonite Voluntary Service, an organization people joined for one or two years at a time, living together in a household and performing service in a location somewhere in the United States or Canada. Many Mennonites did such service just after high school or college. I know Mennonites who met their spouses in MVS.

For our food allowances for each household we used poverty guidelines established by the U.S. government. While this was difficult at times, the fact that we pooled our resources, had gardens, and bought in bulk when we could made living on these guidelines less difficult than most families living in poverty.

Despite this setup and the restrictions on our buying power, we still faced the power of our consumer culture. As Stanley

Hauerwas has written, "If you want to know the power of the demonic, try not being a consumer." We lived in town as families and singles. Most of us worked in various jobs. We were not separated on a commune in the country. I still lusted after books, though my ability to purchase many was severely compromised.

Yes, we felt tensions. But being together strengthened us. We also depended on prayer and worship. We were not trying to follow an ideology but the Lord Jesus. We tried not to depend on the power of ideas but on the power of the Spirit.

The three couples who began NCF told about their efforts to seek peace and justice and practice simplicity. They resisted paying war taxes, marched in peace rallies, and visited prisoners. Meanwhile their marriages were strained—some, they said, about to fall apart. Then they drove in a van to Evanston, Illinois, where Reba Place Fellowship hosted a conference on community. There they witnessed the power of worship and spoke with some of Reba's leaders. On the way back to Newton, they "fell in love" and decided to begin a Christian fellowship modeled after Reba Place and live together in the same neighborhood. While they didn't stop all their peace and justice activities, they focused more on prayer and loving one another. Soon others came and joined them, including me.

Lest I appear to romanticize this period, let me add that NCF made mistakes—at times gave too much authority to a few leaders, was too rigid in its practices when flexibility would have been healthier, took in individuals with mental illness that the pastors were not prepared to handle, and was at times less than generous with people who left the common treasury. And in the end, that way of doing church ended, done in partly by the principalities and powers we tried to oppose and in part by our own mistakes and weakness.

Now the church, today called New Creation Fellowship Church (NCFC), continues and looks like most other Mennonite congregations. But we try to keep alive that element of Mennonite spirituality that says we cannot follow Jesus alone.

We need one another. And we try to practice some politics, some joint decision-making, though it doesn't apply as broadly to our lives as it did.

Our stated mission as a church is to worship God. All else flows from that. And such worship is a political act, even though it may seem innocuous to a world that pays us no attention anyway. In our worship we confess that the Triune God is our ruler. Our allegiance is to God, not other powers that try to claim our worship.

That we worship God and state that as our priority is no guarantee that we live out that allegiance faithfully. We continually fail, yet we believe that God offers forgiveness and the power of presence to help us be faithful. When we gather at the Lord's Table on the first Sunday of each month, we come with thanksgiving (Eucharist) for Jesus' presence, with hunger for healing as we partake of the bread and cup and with confession that we cannot make it on our own. And we come not merely as individuals but as a body.

As a political community, Mennonites practice patience to make peace in the world.

Chapter Five

Play

My work is loving the world.
—Mary Oliver, "Messenger"

Play? How dare I title a chapter in a book on Mennonite spirituality "Play"! After all, Mennonites don't play, do they?

I agree that Mennonites are marked more by work than play (though they do play). Consequently this chapter may involve more prescription than description of Mennonite spirituality. My point: Mennonites—all of us—need to play. It is how God made us, and spirituality—walking in the way of the Spirit—is primarily being who we are, which, I will argue, is a form of play.

Webster's has many definitions of "play" (I'm focusing on the verb). These include engaging in sport or recreation, having sex, moving aimlessly about, taking advantage, performing music, taking part in a game, gaining approval. While playing can be as strenuous as any work we do, we generally distinguish it from working, which usually involves producing something.

Certainly play can be productive. Athletes, musicians, and many others make their living by playing. But I'm using play more in the sense of nonproductive activity, something done for its own sake. I may even call it useless activity, which sounds anathema to many Christians (especially Mennonites), who have a pragmatic bent. But I don't really believe play is useless; it only seems that way to most people.

I've already mentioned (in Chapter One) how Mennonites love to accomplish things, which we'd call work. And they even volunteer in droves to do it.

But play? That's another story. Mennonites tell Mennonite jokes (I imagine the same ones exist in other traditions) about their refusal to engage in play or pleasure. For example, Mennonites don't have sex standing up because it might seem like dancing. Or: Always take two Mennonites with you fishing. If you take one, he'll drink all your beer.

Increasingly, Mennonites do play. I know of Mennonites involved in just about any recreational activity—from biking to sailing to motorcycling to fishing to hunting (yes, with guns) to wine tasting and on and on.

Mennonites also are increasingly involved in the arts—writing, music, painting, sculpture, acting, filmmaking, even dancing. I go to Mennonite writing conferences and find an array of talent and interest. I write a column called "Mediaculture" and include capsule film reviews. I hear from many Mennonites who are passionate about films.

But let's go back to how Mennonite spirituality includes play. Much of what I've mentioned—recreation and the arts—can be interpreted as Mennonites simply assimilating the broader culture. Where do Mennonites get beyond their penchant for productivity or pragmatism? Where do they lose themselves in an activity that feels spiritual?

One such activity is singing. I've witnessed it; I've experienced it. Being in a group of Mennonites singing a hymn in four-part harmony can be a powerful experience.

It can also be off-putting. Mennonites take pride (our Achilles heel) in our singing and maybe sometimes show off. I've felt uncomfortable on a plane full of Mennonites returning from a conference when they break out into "Praise God from Whom All Blessings Flow" (known by many as 606, its number in the *Mennonite Hymnal*, published in 1969). It seems the only way they feel comfortable witnessing to the other passengers. It doesn't feel like loving as much as like boasting. But singing the same song in a conference with several thousand others at the end of a week of worshipping together can be exhilarating.

That act of singing can involve surrender to God and to one another in a communal act of harmony. And while it fills us with joy or peace or whatever, we do it, like all good play, for the glory of God. And like good play, it comes out of who we are. We express with skill and passion thanksgiving for God's gift—in this case of music and one another.

But I don't want to limit play—even so-called spiritual play—to activities considered religious, such as singing hymns. Whatever we do—whether it is recreational activities or even what we call work—can be play. And perhaps it should be.

In whatever we do, we can surrender ourselves to that task and do it to the best of our ability. In doing so, we live in that moment, offering thanks to God for our ability by using it, and likely experiencing a form of joy. It should not need mentioning (but I will) that this is not an absolute rule. Not all activities are good or even acceptable. I suppose a torturer could surrender to his task, do it well and even enjoy it, but it's plainly wrong.

Let it flow

In his book *Flow: The Psychology of Optimal Experience*, Mihaly Csikszentmihalyi describes a quality of enjoyable experience that occurs when a person's ability to act is balanced by challenges to that ability. I think of when I played tennis in high school. It was most enjoyable when I played against someone at about the same skill level I had. Playing someone much worse (which didn't happen often) or playing someone much better (which happened more often) was less enjoyable.

When we're fully engaged in an activity (of body or mind), Csikszentmihalyi writes, we lose self-consciousness, which "can lead to self-transcendence, to a feeling that the boundaries of our being have been pushed forward." The desire to improve the quality of our experience exists in all cultures. As Csikszentmihalyi points out, "Art, play and ritual probably occupy more time and energy in most cultures than work."

Two obstacles to such flow, Csikszentmihalyi writes, are anomie and alienation. Anomie, or lack of rules, is functionally equivalent to attentional disorders, when people cannot give order to their consciousness, and anxiety reigns. Alienation is equivalent to self-centeredness, when "people are constrained by the social system to act in ways that go against their goals." No rules or too many rules are both harmful to experiencing flow. We in the church could learn from this.

"Flow" is a psychological description that can be read as a self-help aid: Here is how to improve your quality of life. However, if we approach an activity with that in mind, flow won't happen because we're too self-conscious.

This relates to the spiritual practice I'm suggesting in this book of living in the present. Play is another way of looking at this, a lens, as it were.

Here we should pay heed to Jesus: Learn from children. When my son Ethan was about twelve, he and friends began digging a hole in our backyard. They created connecting rooms in the hole as it grew over the years. They worked hard, but it was really creative play. Their hours of labor seemed less like what we may think of as work and more like hours of joy.

Play is without goals other than to engage in play. Children don't say, Hey, it would improve our health if we played tag. Neither do they say, Let's play chess because it may improve my mental powers and help me get into a good college.

Unfortunately, we adults increasingly push children into goal-oriented play. When I was growing up, we neighborhood kids made up games. Either we played war (remember, I didn't grow up in a Mennonite context) or, if we had enough playmates who were interested, football or baseball, or, if we were boys and girls, Old Gray Wolf (a form of Hide and Seek). Today, for various reasons, perhaps primarily that both parents (if there are two parents) work away from home, kids' activities are organized by the local recreation center or baseball league or whatever. These can be good activities, but the spontaneity of creating one's own games is gone.

How then should we play? We can enter activities we enjoy—whether basketball, sewing, doing crosswords, or cooking—with a sense of enjoying that activity for itself. This is called autotelic behavior. You can also call it having fun. One way you know you're doing it is when you lose track of time.

But we can also practice this approach to whatever we're doing, even work. Let's say I'm doing the dishes. Many people I know have automatic dishwashers, so this activity involves rinsing the dishes and putting them in the machine. Okay, but for me it means filling one tub with soapy water and one with rinse water, washing each dish with a rag or brush, then rinsing each one and placing it in the rack to air dry.

This is not an especially challenging activity (though it can be at times) or one I get a big kick out of. Nevertheless, I can enter the activity with attentiveness, choosing how I organize the work, making sure I get each dish clean. This is a form of play. It can also be a way to be present in the moment God has given me. Brother Lawrence prayed, "Lord of all pots and pans and things . . . make me a saint by getting meals and washing up the plates" (*Practicing the Presence of God*).

Zen what?

I understand that such "being in the present"—often called mindfulness in Buddhist-related teaching—is a popular notion today. I don't pretend to be original in proposing this. I also don't want merely to jump on a bandwagon. Instead I'm trying to glean wisdom from Christian—and more specifically Mennonite—spirituality, which includes the importance of living in the present, and in God's presence. But I also feel free to draw on wisdom from other traditions. After all, as many Calvinists like to point out, all truth is God's truth.

Why not learn from Zen Buddhism's emphasis on mindfulness? This is translatable into a Christian context. "Zen" means sitting, which is a good way to learn being present.

While Buddhism (pick your kind; there are hundreds of sects) is a long and complex tradition, with strong teaching on compassion and self-sacrifice, much popular writing today on mindfulness has an easy-as-1-2-3 quality to it and tends to focus on oneself. Here's how to be happy, it proclaims.

I don't mean to disparage such a goal. Who doesn't want to be happier? I'm trying to distinguish Christian teaching, which takes such a practice in a different direction. We are not only individuals created in God's image, we are communal beings, made to be in relationship with others. We are created in the image of the Triune God, which has love as its essence. (I don't like that "its," but language fails here, as it often does when discussing God's triune nature, and since English does not have a gender-neutral personal pronoun.) Thus our living in the present is not a way to be happier or feel more fulfilled, though it may have that effect. It is a practice of love, bringing glory to God as we attend to the reality of the moment God has given.

This can quickly feel muddled. Are we supposed to think about all this stuff as we try to live in the moment and do dishes with a sense of play? Not really, for as soon as we do we're not being fully present in that activity. But seeing this context may help us in our practice. If we understand and believe that we are made by a loving God to be in loving relationship, in all that we do—not just "religious" activities but anything, from brushing our teeth to getting dressed—then we can enter each moment with a freedom, a sense of play, knowing we cannot impress God with our good deeds or push God away with our bad deeds.

I hear the objections. So bad deeds don't matter? We shouldn't practice good deeds? Ethics is a complex subject, and I don't pretend to be any kind of expert. My point here is that in practicing Gelassenheit, or self-surrender, we learn to act out of who we are, in the power of God's Spirit, unselfconsciously.

Habitual practices

Our experience in a community of Christians, learning to follow Jesus in various contexts, failing in our efforts yet finding forgiveness—all this shapes us over time. We gradually learn how to connect our life—our story—with the life of the Triune God—God's story.

Such practices (generosity, loving service, self-sacrifice) become more habitual through practice. While we always tend to act out of who we are, we pray that who we are gradually is transformed more and more into the image of Christ—we become more like Jesus (see Chapter Seven). And remember that the chief way we are to "imitate Jesus" (see Chapters One and Two) is through "kenosis," not taking power for ourselves but relinquishing it for God's glory.

And thus we are back to acting in the present moment not out of ego but unselfconsciously. As James McClendon writes about Jesus' parable in Matthew 25, "The King's judgment is based not on their deliberate decisions, if any, but on their unreckoned generosity, their uncaculating love, their 'aimless' faithfulness" (*Ethics*).

As we focus on each moment, the place we are, we focus less on self. Brother Lawrence, a Carmelite monk in the seventeenth century and one of many helpful teachers on this practice, mentions purifying one's life, asking forgiveness from God, being faithful to this practice, focusing on God, using short prayers, mortifying the senses.

For centuries, Christians have promoted various spiritual disciplines, including fasting, prayer, confession, works of mercy, and many more. All these serve to help free us of the ego's powerful hold, help us focus on what is in front of us.

Play, in other words, requires practice, requires discipline, which means learning. Think of a basketball team (I like to think of the 2008 national champion Kansas Jayhawks), which practices every day learning skills so well play becomes instinctual, strengthening the players' endurance to maintain energy even into overtime. The players become a good team as they focus less on themselves and more on the team.

Our spiritual practice, which I'm promoting as play, also requires practice to perfect it. And as we practice we act less out of ego than out of love, which the Spirit gives like breath to breathe in.

Other things contribute to less focus on ego. Suffering often fulfills that function. Richard Rohr calls suffering and prayer "the two great paths of transformation" (*Everything Belongs*). Suffering gets our attention. This is not to imply that God gives us suffering to make us better (though some teach this); it just happens. Also, I don't mean to glorify suffering or revel in it (a la Mel Gibson's film *The Passion of the Christ*).

This talk (writing) of living in the moment, freeing ourselves of our ego through spiritual practices and suffering can sound both formulaic and privileged. I want to avoid the former by saying there is no formula; it's really a mystery.

As to such teaching coming from a position of privilege, such criticism has some validity. I would not dream of trying to offer this message to a child dying of malnutrition, to a mother unable to find enough potable water to care for herself or her children, to a young man dying from AIDS. Such situations demand our attention, our compassion, our action.

I am addressing people with access to this book, who likely share in many of the privileges I possess. Perhaps we can learn together. I also approach this out of my own situation. As I write, Jeanne, my wife, is fighting cancer (thymoma) and living with poor eyesight (likely from a rare toxic reaction to an antibiotic she was on to care for a bacterial infection in her lungs). Each of us lives with uncertainty, anxiety about what may happen. Yet I believe we need to focus on the present, on the Presence of God, who is love, and live there as best we can.

I've given ego a bad rap, but don't we need a healthy sense of self? We're not some amorphous blob, are we, that just sits by passively? No, we're not a blob. We're created in God's image. And play, as I've tried to describe it, is not passive at all. It's to be active and unselfconscious.

False self, true self

I like to return every so often to the writings of Thomas Merton, the Trappist monk who wrote many books from the Gethsemani monastery in Kentucky in the mid-twentieth century and who had a great impact on my life. In one of my favorite of Merton's books, *New Seeds of Contemplation*, he writes about our false self and our true self. "Every one of us is shadowed by an illusory person: a false self," Merton writes. Such a self is the person we may want to be but cannot exist because God does not know that person. And (I love this quote) "to be unknown of God is altogether too much privacy."

Merton goes on to identify this false self with "egocentric desires," with a "thirst for experiences, for power, honor, knowledge and love." But this self is only a kind of packaging without substance. It only hides our "nakedness and emptiness and hollowness."

Our true self, on the other hand, "is hidden in the love and mercy of God," Merton writes. "If I find [God] I will find myself, and if I find my true self I will find [God]."

This false self-true self distinction can veer dangerously close to a kind of Gnosticism that denies the body and all its desires while lifting up some special knowledge. I don't think that's what Merton is saying. He reflects a long Christian mystical tradition (see Teresa of Avila, *The Cloud of Unknowing* and many others) that says as we go deeper within ourselves and release our attachment to outward things to give us meaning, things like material comfort, financial success, acclaim from others (make your own list), we discover God's loving presence. "Those who want to save their life will lose it," says Jesus (Mark 8:35).

Such detachment from other things—comfort, pleasure, status—can lead us into a freedom in God, a sense of finding our true self. Such freedom provides a sense of play. Picture a young girl twirling around, her eyes closed, feeling the breeze on her skin and smelling the flowers surrounding her. Play is to be in that dance each moment, no matter what we're doing.

Earlier I called such play "having fun," which will sound frivolous to many Mennonites (and others). Play cannot be tied to meaningful activity, can it, other than some utilitarian purpose such as exercise or recreation? Well, many Mennonites have fun at hymn sings. I've had fun preaching, and I imagine many other preachers have as well. Even so-called religious activities can be play. Perhaps they're even experienced more fully when done as play.

But I want to extend this further. If nothing we do—even preaching and prayer and singing hymns—impresses God, i.e. makes God love us more, then let's devote all we do to God. And let's do it joyfully, playfully, recognizing that our ability to do it and the moment we do it in are God's gifts to us.

Paul writes to the Roman churches "not to think of yourself more highly than you ought to think, but to think with sober judgment, each according to the measure of faith that God has assigned" (Rom. 12:3). Paul goes on to describe gifts of the Spirit and their use in building up the church.

It's a bit of a paradox, but let me suggest we use sober judgment to not take ourselves too seriously. To play is to lose ourselves, to join others in a dance, each of us performing our steps in time to the music. It's the dance, not us, that matters.

I like to dance—something that distinguishes me from many Mennonites—though I don't do it often. But when I do, I especially enjoy it when I get caught up in the music and don't have to think about the steps. That joy is enhanced when I'm not self-conscious about what others think about dance and when I'm not concerned about how well I might be doing. On August 1, 2009, my daughter Abri got married. At the reception, she and I danced to the song "Father and Daughter," by Paul Simon. Our relationship and the joyous occasion further enhanced the joy of the dance.

Send in the clowns

Henri Nouwen writes that

clowns show us by their "useless" behavior, not simply that many of our preoccupations, worries, tensions and anxieties need a smile, but more important that we, too, have white on our faces and that we, too, are called to clown a little. (*Clowning in Rome*)

I did some clowning back in my early thirties, and it taught me some lessons about play. One lesson has to do with performance. I dressed as a clown to be seen by others, to act in front of them. The time I best remember was for the annual county fair parade in downtown Newton one August. The Newton Area Peace Center, which I helped develop in the early 1980s, had a float in the parade, and a dozen or so of us marched along with it. I dressed as a clown and handed flowers to the people gathered along the street to watch the parade. We had collected the flowers from a dumpster behind a local flower shop over the two previous evenings. We decided to hand out beauty rather than sugar (other groups tossed candy to the crowd).

In that clown outfit I felt like a different person. I acted differently from my usual self, less reserved, more exuberant. I felt responsible to represent clowns everywhere, to show special attention to children (who showed me special attention), to express joy. I also felt a remarkable boldness. In one spontaneous, crazy moment I went up to a police officer directing traffic and kissed him on the cheek. In another circumstance, I suppose I could have been charged with assaulting a cop, but what could he do? I was a clown. At the end of the parade route, a group of cars came by—one of the floats or entries—their young drivers revving the engines loudly. I held my white-gloved hands to my ears, frowned and mimed, "Too loud." It didn't stop the noise pollution; it probably just egged them on, but the clown tried to confront a wrong.

In his book *Performing the Faith*, Stanley Hauerwas argues that Christian witness is to be a performance that is truthful and peaceable, nonviolent. Clowning helps reinforce the notion that we perform, we act out our faith before the world—wherever and whenever we are.

Clowning is both work and fun. It takes time to dress the part, and that costume became uncomfortable on that hot August day. But the freedom and joy of clowning is unforgettable.

Then there's the white face, which Nouwen mentions. Historically this represented a mask of death, and the clown represented one who had died and was resurrected. That's where the freedom comes in. You can't kill the clown, because he or she is already dead. In medieval courts a jester could make comments critical of the king and get away with it. That was part of his role.

The white face, then, leads us to reflect on death, the ultimate detachment, which leads us to freedom. As the poet W. H. Auden has written, "Life is the destiny you are bound / to refuse until you / have consented to die" ("For the Time Being"). We cannot live fully or meaningfully, in other words, until we have faced our mortality. As Jesus told his followers, you cannot live unless you consent to die (carry your cross, which was not a burden but an instrument for the torture and execution of political criminals in ancient Rome).

This may sound morbid, but it's perfectly realistic. We find freedom as we acknowledge the reality that we will die. And in life or death, God is present with us.

Clowning creatively combines these elements—life, death, freedom—and does so in a spirit of play, showing that play is anything but frivolous.

In clowning, too, we lose ourselves in another character, really just another guise. I find this idea helpful as I try to live in each moment.

The truth of fiction

Another form of play for me is fiction. I love to read it and occasionally write it. This, too, has taught me much about play as loving the world.

At times in my work at *The Mennonite*, I've had Mennonite readers say I shouldn't discuss or recommend fiction because it is "just lies." I'm tempted to reply (but usually don't because, I think, What good would it do?) that often there is more truth in fiction than in nonfiction. As novelist Ron Hansen has written, "Fiction holds up to the light, fathoms, simplifies and refines those existential truths that, without such interpretation, seems all too secret, partial and elusive" (*A Stay Against Confu-*

sion). In fiction, you often get into a character's heart and mind and find parallels to your own in a way that simple reporting cannot do.

While fiction can serve as an escape, an entry into another world (as is prayer, I will argue in the next chapter), it also confronts us with the real world and our place in it. Hansen quotes John Gardner, who writes that great fiction "helps us know what to believe, reinforces those qualities that are noblest in us, leads us to feel uneasy about our faults and limitations."

In *The Brothers Karamazov*, one of the greatest novels ever written, we encounter Ivan, the atheist who laments his lack of faith and confronts our easy belief, and Alyosha, whose innocence and simple faith challenges our lackadaisical morality. Doestoevsky even shows a conflict within the monastery, "between the rigid, authoritarian, self-righteous ascetic Therapont," writes Thomas Merton in *Contemplative Prayer*,

> who delivers himself from the world by sheer effort, and then feels qualified to call down curses upon it; and the Staretz, Zossima, the kind, compassionate man of prayer who identifies himself with the sinful and suffering world to call down God's blessing upon it.

I first read this novel in high school as a young Christian and have read it since. Each time I feel confronted by the questions it raises and inspired by Father Zossima. It doesn't matter that it is set in nineteenth-century Russia, a world far removed from my own. It affects me on several levels—intellectual, emotional, ethical, philosophical. And its subject, ultimately, is love, the theme that enfolds us all and lies at the heart of play and of spirituality.

Writing fiction lures one even deeper into the subtle power of imagination, God's gift, after all. But regarding the tension I've described between accepting the real and pursuing the ideal, fiction writing takes one in a bit different direction. As Flannery O'Connor has written, fiction writers' only objective is to be "hotly in pursuit of the real."

Didacticism, teaching a lesson, is death to good fiction, which brings us face to face with the real. O'Connor writes that "what is good in itself glorifies God because it reflects God. The artist has his hands full and does his duty if he attends to his art."

Nevertheless, fiction does not merely describe what's real, since what's real includes much more than any surface description. Writing is a sacrament, Hansen writes, when it gives readers "the feeling that life has great significance, that something is going on here that matters."

Writing fiction has taught me about love—and maybe a little about God. When I create characters, I realize they're most alive—real and complex—when I love them. Flat characters, those with only one trait, whether good or evil, or who seem stereotypical, a type that represents all people of that kind, according to small-minded people, ruins a story. These are the characters you often see in genre fiction or certain movies, where the bad guys are always bad and wear black, while the good guys are always good and wear white, where the woman is always a helpless victim and the man is either the victimizer or the rescuer. Or, looking at many movies for the adolescent crowd, teenagers are always smart, and adults are always dumb.

It's hard to love flat characters; they just aren't real. But complex characters, not all bad or all good, are both created out of love and are easy to love. We care about them because they feel real. And such characters can seem to take over the creative process.

In the early 1990s, I wrote a historical novel (unpublished) based loosely on the time period and events in the life of my great-grandfather Barney Houser. Much of the book is about Seth Paxson, the fictional character based loosely on Barney. I had an outline, a plan to write the novel in three parts. But I did not plan to write the second part in first-person, narrated by Seth's wife, Emily. That idea came out of the blue and took hold of me. I decided to try it, and writing that part of the novel gave me perhaps the greatest challenge and greatest joy of the entire process of writing that novel.

In writing fiction I've had to learn to portray characters unlike me, even characters I don't like. Yet as I create them I grow to love them, as they move beyond being ciphers to being real, complex characters. Maybe that provides a hint, only a hint, of the love of God, who created each of us.

Writing, another form of play, helps us move out of ourselves in an act of love—love for beauty and order and complexity—as we create another world.

Perhaps you've had this experience—and if not you'll likely think me weird, if you haven't already. You watch a movie, in which every movement is carefully planned, every speech scripted, and afterward you find yourself acting more deliberately, even more smoothly, as you go about your tasks, whether it's drinking a cup of tea or taking out the trash. It's as if you're watching yourself, and you feel calm, and time slows down.

On the one hand, this shows the powerful effect of film—a medium that engages our senses of sight and sound and our emotions and intellect—to alter our behavior. As a child I'd watch a TV show or movie about World War II, then go outside and play war. Many argue about the effects on our behavior of viewing violence, others the effects of viewing ads. Such viewing affects us, though to what extent depends, I would argue, on many factors. As a sometime film reviewer, I encourage people to think about what they've just seen, if possible talk about it with others. I believe this mitigates the effects of that medium, helps objectify it. It's similar to the spiritual practice of discernment, looking at a situation and seeking God's perspective, which we can only glimpse, but what is more objective?

Back to my experience of slowing down, acting more deliberately after watching a film: I'm less interested in using film to reach that experience than in that experience itself, which gives us a hint of living in the present.

Each year in our magazine, I record my top ten films of the previous year. My No. 1 film of 2007 was an obscure documentary, made by a German and set in the French Alps. This almost three-hour film, called *Into Great Silence*, filmed monks at a

Carthusian monastery as they went through their day, praying (often), singing, preparing meals, cleaning, even cutting other monks' hair. The director used no voiceover, no music other than the chanting of the monks, but most of the film is simply showing these monks living their ordinary yet remarkable, silent lives.

Sounds terribly boring, right? In some ways, yes. But the pace of the film and its subject matter have a hypnotic effect on the viewer. For me, it went deeper. After viewing it, I felt my life had changed. I felt more at peace and moved slower, with less anxiety about what I was getting done. Each thing I did seemed significant. I went to the kitchen that evening (I watched the film on DVD; it never came to a theater near me) and put away the dishes from the drainer. It felt like prayer. I chose this film as my No. 1 not because it was the best, most artistic film of 2007 but because it affected me more than any other film.

Again, I'm not recommending that we use this film (you may hate it) or another to help us slow down and live in the present, i.e. play. I am suggesting that we find practices that help us play, that help free us from the dominance of our ego. Such practices will help us live patiently, peaceably, and in harmony with others. They will help us attend to and love the world God has made in the moments God gives us.

Chapter Six

Prayer

It is far more valuable to speak to God than to speak about God, for there is so much self-love in spiritual conversations.
—Therése of Lixieux

Prayer, like play, is considered useless. While play at least can give you exercise your body needs, prayer accomplishes nothing. It is, according to many, a delusional activity, talking to someone who's not there.

Yet millions of people across the planet pray every day—from highly ritualized communal prayers to ecstatic utterances accompanied by bodily reactions (such as being "slain in the Spirit") to intercessions for suffering loved ones to the desperate "God, help me" mutterings of someone in trouble who rarely "prays" otherwise. The majority of people pray in some way.

So are most people crazy? The so-called "new atheists" who enjoy mocking belief (usually a fundamentalist form of Christianity) operate on their own set of beliefs—that there is no God, that somehow something came from nothing, that all these believers are fools.

But I don't wish to debate the new atheists. Many others have done a good job of that. My point is that prayer represents a yearning for help beyond ourselves. We live in our limited world and long for eternity. We live with immanence and long for transcendence. And as Augustine famously put it, "We cannot rest until we find our rest in [God]" (*Confessions*).

Prayer is certainly a part of Mennonite spirituality, though most would not place "Mennonites" and, say, "contemplative prayer" in the same sentence. Some have called their hymnals the Mennonites' prayer books. And singing, as I've mentioned, is where Mennonites have their keenest experiences of transcendence, of a Reality beyond themselves.

This is not just a Mennonite phenomenon. From its earliest days as Jewish followers of Jesus of Nazareth, whom its members called "Messiah" and "Lord," the church has sung "psalms and hymns and spiritual songs" (Eph. 5:19). Singing, as I've written, is a form of play that can take us out of ourselves, unite us with others and give glory to God.

Singing, then, is one form of prayer, which takes many forms, which is a kind of play. Then why include a chapter on prayer? I almost didn't. I argued with myself like this:

Self 1: Just include it with "Play," since it can fit there. Besides, that gives you seven chapters, the perfect number.

Self 2: Yes, but how can you write a book on spirituality and not include a chapter on prayer? After all, it starts with P, and besides, eight is my favorite number. (It's also significant; see the eighth day of creation.)

Self 1: But it's such a huge topic that everybody and his brother (or sister) has written about. What do you have to say that's new? You're no expert.

Self 2: That's for sure, but then I'm no expert on any of this stuff, which I've tried to make clear. You're right about its being a huge topic, but it's important to me.

Self 1: What about the quote from St. Thérése?

Self 2: Point taken. But I'm a fool, and we're supposed to be willing to take risks, right?

Self 1: I agree with the first part.

Self 2: Okay, then pray for me.

So here we go. Mennonites pray—through singing, spoken prayers, in small groups, individually. Some even pray in tongues. Lately many (including me) are using morning and evening prayers from prayer books (see Arthur Paul Boers' *The*

Rhythm of God's Grace). Mennonites have even produced their own prayer book (*Take Our Moments and Our Days,* the first in a series). Of course, they call it an Anabaptist prayer book, I suppose so they don't scare off outsiders.

Some Mennonites have been in dialogue with Catholics through a group called Bridgefolk, which Jeanne and I have participated in. To oversimplify, Mennonites want to draw on the wisdom of Catholics regarding spirituality, while Catholics want to draw on the wisdom of Mennonites regarding peacemaking. The meetings I've attended have been rich, with much give and take, learning from one another and finding ways to connect.

In one of those meetings, C. Arnold Snyder, a Mennonite historian, spoke about the prayer practices of sixteenth-century Anabaptists. He noted the predominance of Scripture in their prayers. But then, anyone who's used the Daily Office knows that it's mostly Scripture excerpts. Those in the Anabaptist prayer book, however, seem more weighted toward helping believers obey their call to follow Jesus.

What is prayer?

But before we go further, what is prayer? We all have our ideas about it, and most of us who believe it's important feel we fall short in our practice of it. There are basic definitions, such as communication with God, but I like this, from an anonymous twentieth-century Christian hermeticist (hermit):

> Prayer—which asks, thanks, worships and blesses—is the radiation, the breath and the warmth of the awakened heart: expressed in formulae of the articulated word, in the wordless inner sighing of the soul and, lastly, in the silence, both outward and inward, of the breathing of the soul immersed in the element of divine respiration and breathing in unison with it. (*Watch and Pray: Christian Teachings on the Practice of Prayer*)

What I like about this definition is that it includes the basics ("asks, thanks, worships, and blesses"), is poetic ("the radiation, the breath and the warmth of the awakened heart"), includes but does not limit itself to use of words ("the wordless inner sighing of the soul"), and expresses one of this book's major themes: surrendering to God's action ("immersed in the element of divine respiration").

All I can add is commentary on this, using thoughts from many other wise practitioners and relating some of my own feeble experiences.

For a long time I've had a great interest in prayer (I'm an introvert, remember?), but I've done more reading about prayer than actual praying. I try to console myself that I pray the Daily Office (just the morning and evening prayers, using *Celebrating Common Prayer*) on most days. I pray for a list of people—family, friends, some enemies, even Mennonite Church USA—each day, but I tend to rush through it, usually without much feeling, except when I pray for Jeanne and my children, Ethan and Abri. I even try to meditate twice a day, but I fail miserably, my mind wandering. I also see a spiritual director, a Mennonite pastor trained in spiritual direction, who is a great listener and encourages me, but I could put more effort into it from my end.

So you see, Self 1 is right. I'm far from being an expert. Nevertheless, I plod on.

Many Christians (Mennonites included) see prayer as a duty that they mostly fail at. Perhaps nothing induces more guilt in a Christian than asking, How's your prayer life? We know it's important, yet we find it so difficult. Why?

Perhaps in part it's the conflict Merton describes as underlying all Christian conversion: "the turning to a freedom based no longer on social approval and relative alienation but on direct dependence on an invisible and inscrutable God" (*Contemplative Prayer*).

We may know much about prayer—that it includes praise, thanksgiving, confession, intercession, and even silence—but that doesn't always help us pray. And we think of prayer as something we must set aside time for. But we're not monks. We have jobs, plus chores at home. Then we need some time to relax, maybe watch the tube or check our email. Soon it's time for bed, then up the next day for more of the same. Who has time for prayer? we ask, though we know in our hearts that if it were really important, we'd make time.

Pray without ceasing

Then there's the strange admonition to "pray without ceasing" (1 Thess. 5:17). What in the world can that mean?

Two approaches face us, both of which I want to avoid while actually combining them. A contradiction? Probably, but the more I delve into spirituality, the more contradiction (we'll call it paradox) I find. Another word for it is mystery, which certainly applies to prayer.

One approach is to push you, Dear Reader, to get off your butt (or maybe onto it) and practice prayer more faithfully. Stop making excuses and just do this important task. And here are some helpful tips to get you going.

Another approach is to dumb down prayer, to say everything we do can be prayer, so don't sweat it. It's easy really.

I've stated these approaches with bold hyperbole. But each has its truth. We do need to practice prayer, and there are both techniques and ways of understanding prayer that can help us. And, as Thérèse says, it's better to talk to God than about God.

Also, if prayer is only words, then praying without ceasing is an impossibility (maybe Paul was just using hyperbole). We should, I believe, make everything we do a kind of prayer, just as we make it a kind of play. And while that's not easy, it is simple.

Let me go over some perspectives on prayer by reflecting on my own experience.

When I was a new Christian, back in high school, not knowing or in conversation with other Christians besides attending church with my mother, I prayed. Mostly it was the "God, help me" kind of prayer, with some "God, help so-and-so" and some thank-you's. But sometimes it felt strange, like I was talking to myself. Who was this Person I was praying to? I knew so little about him. Yet I knew that I'd given myself to God because I knew I couldn't make it on my own.

That dependence—or awareness of dependence—is a basic stance of prayer. We pray not knowing God fully (an impossibility anyway) but humbly believing our life depends on this Person. As Richard Rohr writes, prayer is falling "into the hands of the living God" (Heb. 10:31). Both the falling and the place where we fall are keys to prayer. There has to be a strong element of trust that those hands will catch us and that they are loving hands. That's something we have to keep learning. Falling is never easy. We'd much rather walk on our own power.

What soon tripped me up—and what trips up most of us—was when I prayed fervently for something, and it didn't happen. In the summer following my graduation from high school, one of my classmates (though not a person I knew well) was injured at the Iowa Beef Packing plant where he worked. A co-worker tossed him the stun gun they used to kill cattle by shooting them in the head, and the gun went off and hit my classmate in the head. He was in a coma for nearly a week. Each day the *Emporia Gazette* carried an update on his condition, and each day I prayed he would live. I prayed fervently. He died.

I can look back now and think, *No one survives such an accident.* I was asking a lot—a miracle. And from experience I now know that God does not answer all our requests in the way we wish, no matter how fervently we pray. But for me as a seventeen- (soon to be eighteen-) year-old, that experience was hard. I felt confused and upset. I wanted to be angry at God but wondered, *Can one even do that and still be a Christian?*

Faith crisis

Fourteen years later I had another crisis—similar in kind but somehow more profound. I was at NCF, married to Jeanne and a father to Ethan, who was two and a half. Jeanne and I wanted a second child. We'd already had two miscarriages and were expecting again. Jeanne was nearly twelve weeks along, and we were hoping to get a heartbeat at our next appointment with the ob/gyn doctor. Then Jeanne had some bleeding. We each prayed; we each felt the Lord saying the baby would be okay.

NCF encouraged the practice of "listening to the Lord," which is a concentrated way of praying that involves imagining the Lord (Jesus, the Spirit, however one might image God's voice) giving a person a message. It's not an audible voice but a sense. The church encouraged this practice but also emphasized the need to discern with others whether or not a message was really "from the Lord."

At times such words from the Lord came during a community gathering, either a Sunday morning worship time or a midweek meeting. Such "prophecy" (mentioned in 1 Cor. 12) was seen as a charismatic gift. Another gift was "discernment of spirits" (1 Cor. 12:10), which helped determine if the message was genuine. Such "words" also came to individuals in their private prayer times, either for themselves or for others. These, too, were usually tested.

Jeanne and I each had a sense of the Lord assuring us the baby was fine. As it turned out, however, the baby was already dead. We went to the doctor and learned that the fetus had stopped growing at about eight weeks. On the way home from the doctor's office, I leaned out the car window and yelled to the sky, "You bastard."

I understand this may sound silly to some and blasphemous to others—silly because, obviously, God didn't cause the baby to die, and blasphemous because you just don't address God that way. But my shout was not from some rational or cautious side of me but from my heart, my gut. It was a cry of anguish and anger, of feeling loss and feeling betrayed. At that point I experienced a loss of faith—in my own ability to hear God's voice and in the God I prayed to.

As I was to discover later, I did not lose my faith in God but in the image of God I carried within me. And I still believed enough to yell at him.

I stopped praying. What was the use? I thought. God didn't answer my most heartfelt prayer. Why pray at all? It would seem false, merely going through motions, dishonest. I told my small group and others in NCF what I felt. They didn't judge me but said, We will have faith for you. One of the most meaningful responses for me came from my close friend Vicki, who does not use "colorful" language. When she heard the news, she said, "Shit!" At that moment I felt such empathy from her. She understood. And I felt relief that my crisis of faith was not going to bring down others. This gave me freedom to experience it fully.

The next few months were dark. I fell into a depression, though I was able to continue my job. But I was a lousy husband, offering little support to Jeanne, who was dealing with her own grief. That fall we decided to dissolve the common treasury, which affected Jeanne more than me, since she was the bookkeeper. (NCF Inc. had just paid over $40,000 to IRS after a three-year audit of our 1980-81 returns, and now the 1982-83 returns were being audited. NCF had sold four houses to get the money. Now we had no assets but the houses we lived in.)

Also, we agreed to let the fifteen-year-old daughter of a couple in the common treasury who had moved to Reba Place come live with us that school year. She ended up being a godsend in many ways because of the attention she gave Ethan while his parents were barely coping.

Two things (outside the support of our church) helped turn me around. One was a letter from Richard Rohr, whom I'd stayed with a couple of days in 1977, when he was a leader at New Jerusalem Community in Cincinnati. Later he founded the Center for Action and Contemplation in Albuquerque, New Mexico. We had corresponded occasionally, and I saw him a couple of times when he was leading retreats in Wichita. During that fall of 1985, I wrote him and described my loss of faith. On October 2, he wrote me one of the most beautiful letters I've ever received. Full of empathy and affirmation, the letter said that God was inviting me to "a deeper Center, . . . your true Center where you are grounded in the Absolute, where *you and He are already One* and already deeply in love" (his emphasis). Richard wrote that I was "created for Absurd Love. The space for it is growing inside you now." He did not promise comfort but said, "The labor pains of Love will probably be long and very real. . . . It is yours to bear."

All I felt was pain, yet Richard said this was part of a process that would actually draw me closer to God, who was not some servant to do my bidding or a fickle tyrant but a Father who created me for Absurd love. The letter lit in me a spark of hope.

A week before I received Richard's letter, I attended a retreat at the Manna House of Prayer in Concordia, Kansas, led by James Finley, a contemplative writer who was a novice under Thomas Merton in the 1960s at Gethsemani. He spoke of God as "the Really Real" who is infinitely present, loving mercy. I spoke with Finley about my inability to pray the prayer of petition (ask God for something). He said we can't make God more present, caring, or merciful by asking, but we may increase our awareness of that care and mercy.

This was helpful, but prayer still seemed too much a fiction. It made no sense to me. For months, all I could pray each day was Psalm 62:1b: "For God alone my soul waits in silence." Everything else seemed false.

The Psalms are the Bible's prayer book, and they're filled with utterances that are so nakedly honest they make us uncomfortable. Various Psalmists pour out their anguish and revel in God's rescue (a word that Robert Alter prefers to salvation, since it's usually a rescue from physical enemies, not some amorphous salvation from sin). Some statements are so shocking we refuse to read them in public, such as rejoicing over those who take the little ones of the Babylonians who had sent Israel into exile and "dash them against the rock" (Ps. 137:9).

Eventually I came to a place of praying for others, even myself, but I did so without any expectation that these prayers would effect a change. I'd learned (whether true or not) that I had no control over what God might do. Yet I'd come to believe that I should be honest in my prayers—tell God what I wanted, confess my shortcomings, express my thanks, and acknowledge my dependence on God for my very breath.

Thus, I pray each day for Jeanne's healing, even though I feel no assurance this will happen, other than the healing God brings ultimately to us after our death. I figure, Why not say what I want? Perhaps this is an outgrowth of the stoicism I inherited from my family. Perhaps it's a way to protect myself from disappointment. My pessimist philosophy has been to expect the worst; then any surprise will be a pleasant one. But I don't always take that approach. I still experience disappointment, which means I was expecting something better.

Desire

In approaching prayer this way, I don't mean to deny my desires, which give energy to my life. As Ronald Rolheiser writes, "Desire is the straw that stirs the drink" (*The Holy Longing*). He then defines spirituality as "what we do with our unrest."

As I outline living in the present, surrendering ourselves to God, not trying to control events or dominate others, I've tried to say that this is not to be equated with passivity. Jesus, a good Jew, was anything but passive. He brought healing to many, gave hope and leadership, confronted powers opposing God's reign, yet he did so out of a deep cooperation with God. The Holy Spirit energized him.

I recognize my own inclination as a Five (in the Enneagram typology) is to detach. And as I've said, this can be good and bad. We are to detach from the domination of our ego or of others but not from the energy of God's Spirit within, not from others we are called to love.

Rolheiser addresses this interplay. Spirituality, he writes, is what we do with the fire that burns in us, what he calls "eros," a Greek word for love. "Spirituality concerns what we do with desire," he writes. "It is about being integrated or falling apart, about being within community or being lonely, about being in harmony with Mother Earth or being alienated from her."

Spirituality, then, is about how we channel our eros. "The opposite of being spiritual," Rolheiser writes, "is to have no energy, is to have lost all zest for living." But that energy is not to be directionless. "A healthy soul keeps us both energized and glued together." An apt description of Jesus, our model for spirituality.

Back in fall 1985 and beyond, I had little zest for living. That "dark night," if that's what it was—maybe it was simple depression—was part of changing the image of God I prayed to. We all pray with a certain image of God that is to some degree false, since God is beyond any of our conceptions. Our talk of God, says Anthony de Mello, is like a finger pointing at the moon. We tend to focus on the finger and neglect the moon.

As I grew closer to a God who seemed less distinct, more mysterious, I grew more able to return the love my brothers and sisters in the church were giving me. I was able to serve again in different ways—in church, my work, and my family. But a certain caution remained, call it a scar from the wound I felt to my faith.

I prayed but focused more on silence and thanksgiving. I became interested in the Daily Office, and after a weeklong retreat at Nova Nada, a Carmelite monastery in Colorado, I began practicing morning and evening prayer using a prayer book. Communion grew in importance for me.

Still, I have much to learn and need to grow. When I read in Rolheiser that a healthy soul "must put some fire in our veins, keep us energized, vibrant, living with zest and full of hope as we sense that life is, ultimately, beautiful and worth living," I realize I'm not completely healthy. But I hope I'm moving in that direction.

He goes on to say that "a healthy soul has to keep us fixed together, . . . give us a sense of who we are, where we came from, where we are going and what sense there is in all of this." In this respect I feel healthier, more integrated.

I don't want to focus only on myself, however. I wonder whether or not many North American Mennonites face this same lack, this need for growth. Are not many of us "fixed together" yet needing fire in our veins and a sense that life is beautiful and worth living?

It is one of many ironies that it is the Mennonites in Latin America, Africa, and Asia, where people often experience greater suffering and persecution, who have this fire, this energy and hope, who have much to teach us.

Why suffering?

Here again that critter "suffering" rears its head. It serves, as I've said, to get our attention, to help ease the grip of our ego, to help us realize we can't make it on our own. Yet it also becomes a stumbling block, a reason to question God's goodness.

How does the immense suffering in our world—the deaths of more than 32,000 children per day from hunger and preventable diseases, for example—square with the prodigal father who lavishes mercy on his wayward son (Luke 15:11-32)?

That question, addressed over the centuries by theodicy (Webster's: the defense of God's goodness and omnipotence in view of the existence of evil), plagues us all to varying degrees and is likely the No. 1 reason given by atheists for not believing in God.

Many of us who believe in God carry on with that question either haunting us or at least prickling the back of our minds. I will not pretend to give an answer but again plead, It's a mystery.

The question itself, as I've framed it, is complex. As Susan Neiman has argued in her alternative history of philosophy, *Evil in Modern Thought*, "Evils come in too many forms to confine." Therefore, she writes, "evils cannot be compared, but they should be distinguished." The "evil" of the Lisbon earthquake of 1755 is not the same as what happened at Auschwitz, which is different from what happened on September 11, 2001. "Getting clear about the differences will not put an end to evil, but it may help prevent our worst reactions to it."

We usually attach "the problem of evil" to religion, but religion, Neiman writes, "no more invented the concept of evil than the concept of good. Religion is rather a way of trying to give shape and structure to the moral concepts that are embedded in our lives."

My point is that we pray in the face of such questions and must live with a certain amount of uncertainty. We come to God, however we come, with a certain view of the One we address. Perhaps we come burdened by guilt and fear God's reprisal. Or we come desperate, as a last measure, when all our efforts have failed. Or we come out of habit yet with doubt, believing God can answer but not sure he will. Perhaps, like me, we've felt burned, our dearest hopes dashed. But, as Peter said to Jesus (John 6:60), Where else can we go?

Jesus seemed to anticipate our fears and misgivings about prayer when he instructed his disciples to "ask, and it will be given you; search, and you will find; knock, and the door will be opened for you" (Luke 11:9). He goes on to say that a human father would not give a snake to a child who asked for a fish, or a scorpion to one who asked for an egg. "If you, then, who are evil, know how to give good gifts to your children, how much more will the heavenly Father give the Holy Spirit to those who ask him!" (Luke 11:13).

Maybe our problem is that we ask for fish and eggs when we should ask for the Holy Spirit. I've prayed and heard many prayers for those who are suffering, and often someone prays that the person experience (feel, know) God's presence.

That's a good prayer, I believe, and fits well with Jesus' teaching, though I continue to ask God to heal Jeanne (as well as my own disabilities) simply because that's what I desire, and only God can do it.

When we ask, How can a good God allow suffering? We need to ask further what we mean by "good," "God," and "suffering." But at least it's not usually an intellectual question but a cry of anguish. I'm hurting because so-and-so is suffering, and I want it to end. Many of us understand God as one who might say, "So do I." We believe God suffers with us.

That is one response, which takes us into the realm of God's immanence. We worship not only the transcendent, all-powerful God but Emmanuel, God-with-us, the one incarnate in Jesus, who himself suffered horribly.

While that is true, it doesn't always answer our anguish. As Nicholas Wolterstorff has written, following the death of his son, "My wound is an unanswered question. The wounds of all humanity are an unanswered question" (*Lament for a Son*).

Suffering is all around us, an obvious part of our world. And it is "a mystery as deep as any in our existence," Wolterstorff writes. Yet it is also tied to love. We suffer at the loss of others because we love them. Therefore, "in commanding us to love, God invites us to suffer."

A deeper mystery, perhaps, is that God suffers. Richard Rohr writes, "If the suffering of Jesus is the image and revelation of the invisible God (Col. 1:15), this is totally at odds with all the other philosophical and theological definitions of a supreme being" (*Job and the Mystery of Suffering*).

The God we pray to also suffers and let Jesus suffer and die. What good is that? As Mark Twain complained, God sees the sparrow fall, but it still falls.

Is our problem less the God who won't take away our suffering—or that of others—than our perception of God and of suffering? My experience led me to see God differently, but I could be wrong. I'm sure I'm still half-blind spiritually.

As I try to practice living in the present, I have to learn to live with what is, to not put off living until things get better. I have to look for what gift might be present with my suffering. I don't like pain, but I understand Rohr's comment that "pain is an activator that forces us to choose between what is important and what is not."

And Jeanne is my teacher as well. As she literally loses her sight, she is understandably frustrated, but her humble submission to God continually amazes me. She wants healing as much or more than anyone, yet she says, "I'm learning to depend on God more, which I need to do." Neither of us believes God caused this to teach her a lesson. But she is learning from what is and drawing closer in her experience of God's presence.

Perhaps suffering is a form of prayer. Wolterstorff points to this when he speaks of "the shout of 'No' by one's whole existence to that over which one suffers." It is a longing for God's final healing of the world.

Rohr calls suffering "sharing in the passion of God . . . participating in what God is going through for the sake of love and union."

If prayer is whatever draws us closer to the heart of God and helps us experience God's presence more fully, then suffering as well as play, laughter, tears, toil, dance, and many other things can be prayer. But all prayer is to be guided and infused by love.

From numbness to depth

While suffering can serve to get our attention, we in North America often face a more lethal problem: a numbness that develops from our exposure to a culture that promotes comfort, satiety, greed and superficial pleasures. In an interview with *National Catholic Reporter* (Aug. 17, 2007), Rolheiser calls American culture "the most powerful narcotic this planet has ever perpetrated."

We imbibe everything from fast food to Soaps to vengeance movies to cosmetic surgery to the NFL. We live on a surface of distractions to deal with the ennui that puts us to sleep. Rolheiser says, "John of the cross warned about over-distracting and numbing ourselves, because then when you face life-changing events you are not ready, you lack the depth."

Perhaps you learn one day that you have cancer and may live only six months. Are you ready for that? Spiritual practices such as prayer help sustain us in the face of such challenges.

We are created with a longing for wholeness, we are born with a cry for air as we enter the cold world from the warm womb. Rolheiser calls that longing "holy," a divine fire that is a source of our creativity and our search for God. But without spiritual disciplines to help us channel this energy into generativity, we often fall into destructive or numbing addictions.

Spirituality is about wholeness, combining aspects of ourselves that seem contradictory. That divine fire within us makes us passionate, yet that passion can be destructive without discipline. Rolheiser says, "The ideal would be powerful passion, powerful purity, powerful enjoyment and powerful responsibility, all at once." When you read "power" in that sense, think Holy Spirit, which combines passion and purity.

When we encounter suffering, then, we can respond in different ways, depending in part on our spiritual training. Suffering can leave us bitter, angry, and imbalanced, or it can make us compassionate, forgiving, and loving.

After that third miscarriage, I felt angry and depressed, but thanks to my church community and some helpful spiritual guides, I also went deeper in my walk with God.

Prayer is one of those disciplines that helps us experience life in greater depth and thus face suffering with greater maturity. Watching TV just won't get us to that depth.

Does that mean we should be praying all the time and never watch TV or eat junk food or any of a dozen other ways we all (with a few exceptions) participate in American culture? If I'm saying that, then you may as well close this book and forget what I wrote earlier about living with what is, not to mention how God made us all so different—with those nine Enneagram types and all the different shapes and possibilities we embody. It also means I'm a bigger hypocrite than I already am, since I watch TV, eat junk food occasionally, and participate in American culture in many ways, as you've no doubt surmised by my references to rock 'n roll, sports, and movies.

We come to God in prayer from where we are, and where we are is smack-dab in the middle of American culture. I've referred to a Mennonite tradition of noncomformity, and while that remains a key element in Mennonite spirituality, it takes a different form today for the most part. Most Mennonites participate in the broader culture in a variety of ways, and like anyone, we are affected by that culture—in good and bad ways. How much we are affected depends partly on how aware we are of its effects.

Here comes that word again—*discernment*. To figure out how our culture affects us requires discernment on many fronts, and we will never be fully aware or free of these effects. A community of fellow pilgrims, so to speak, who share our values and commitments can help us see things we miss (see Chapter Four). Our blind spots abound, and our lenses keep changing, so it's difficult. Prayer and other disciplines can also help us. In these ways we seek to look at ourselves and our world from a different perspective.

Living in another culture, even for a short time, helps us gain a different perspective. Mennonites have made this an emphasis as well. My daughter attends (at the time of this writing) Goshen (Ind.) College, a Mennonite school that requires its students to spend one semester overseas to graduate. Many Mennonites have also served overseas, doing relief and development or mission work. Such activities take these people out of their familiar context and place them in another. There they learn that people are people, but they approach the world from different perspectives. They also learn that people often don't fit our stereotypes of them.

In all these ways we gain a more objective view of our culture and our participation in it. But it's never fully objective; we always come with lenses shaped by our experience.

I'm suggesting, nevertheless, that we practice what spiritual disciplines we can to be more aware, awake to, the presence of God within and around us. Thus, we don't come to God in any spatial sense, since God is ever there—here. We come in the sense of our awareness of that Presence. When we pray—in whatever form that takes—we acknowledge that Presence.

Then when we encounter life-altering events that rip us out of our comfortable, cultural milieu, we can face them with a deeper sense of God's presence.

Back to my earlier question: Should we then be praying all the time? Formally, no. But on some level we seek to, since we are called to pray unceasingly. How does our cultural participation fit with this?

The focus of this book is to encourage living in the present moment, with some awareness of being in the presence of God. This doesn't mean we're always thinking about God. Besides, any such thoughts merely reflect our image of God. Instead we offer each moment to God and live in that moment. Thus, if I'm watching a movie or a TV show, I'm doing this in God's presence. If I'm eating a Big Mac (unlikely, not my cup of tea) or playing miniature golf, I do this in God's presence.

The sticky part is realizing that certain activities can be numbing (to use Rolheiser's term) and affect our awareness of God's energy (fire) within us. Some cultural activities can help us move into that depth of experience that helps our awareness. Others not so much. I like a good mystery—whether in book form or on the screen—as much as most people. I have a particular weakness for spy stories. I understand the desire for escape from the eroding doldrums of everyday life. But we need to mix in some things that challenge us, draw us into questions we may find uncomfortable. There is much good literature (classic and contemporary) and many good films (classic and contemporary), for example, that will draw our imagination into other worlds, where we encounter questions of mortality, ethics, meaning, God, and our place in the world. We may listen as we read books or watch films for what Stephen Prickett has called "whispers of divinity within the machine of language" (quoted in *In the Light of Christ* by Lucy Beckett).

I admit this looking into literature and film is my cup of tea and not everyone's. And this talk of awareness may betray my penchant as a Five for knowledge. Others will find other avenues in our culture for finding challenges to our complacency and support for experiencing God's presence in our lives.

Forms of prayer

Although I want to expand our notion of prayer beyond words and certain forms, it may be helpful to at least look at some of those forms.

We've discussed the prayer of petition, with which I struggled after that third miscarriage. This is a common form, used in our private prayers as we pray for others and ourselves but also in church and in smaller prayer groups. I find this a helpful way to communicate love to one another. We've heard from many people who say they are praying for Jeanne's healing. I find this encouraging, not because fifty people praying will more likely convince God to do something than only twenty-five people praying, but because in praying for Jeanne those people are expressing their love. And being loved by others gives you strength and helps you hope.

There are more advanced or complex ways of praying for one another. One our church uses sometimes is to gather around the person being prayed for and laying hands on him or her. Touch is a powerful way of communicating love to people.

Jeanne has been involved in something called Theophostic (meaning divine light) prayer. She and two women from our congregation regularly get together to pray for each other. Each time they focus on one of the three. This form of praying involves using one's imagination to picture Jesus coming to that person at a time in their past when they experienced a hurt that also damaged their faith, affected their view of God.

As I understand it, and I don't understand it fully, the person being prayed for usually focuses on a certain event and pictures Jesus present there, then attends to what Jesus says or does. Those praying for the person ask questions or restate what they hear the person say. Jeanne has reported some amazing experiences during such prayers, when some unusual imagery turned out to be helpful.

I've already written about thanksgiving as a central aspect of prayer, especially helpful in maintaining an awareness of being in God's presence. In private prayer, we begin with giving thanks—for whatever is going well but mostly for God's presence, which is constant and unaffected by how things are going.

Communion

Corporate thanksgiving is a key element in our worship. In thanksgiving we acknowledge our dependence on God for all that we are and have. Then there's the Eucharist, a word that means thanksgiving, in which we experience the presence of

Christ through the Holy Spirit, giving thanks for Jesus offering his life to the Father, who raised him from the dead.

In some ways, Mennonites' attitudes toward the Eucharist, which they typically call Communion or the Lord's Supper, seem a reaction to the Catholic view of it as a sacrament and the focal point of worship, the Mass. This goes back to the sixteenth century, when Anabaptists broke away from a Catholic Church with numerous problems, then later saw many of their fellow members killed by Catholic authorities. As John Rempel writes, Anabaptist leaders developed their doctrines of the Lord's Supper

> through the controversies which distanced the Anabaptist movement from both (1) sacramentalism (the automatic mediation of grace through priestly power and the elements themselves) and (2) spiritualism (a divorce between the inwardness of religious reality and the outwardness of the material world). (*The Lord's Supper in Anabaptism*)

One has only to read Rempel's book to see that I'm wildly simplifying what was a complex situation. There was not one Anabaptist view of the Lord's Supper, and the ones that emerged had subtle nuances. Also they developed in situations where their authors might be killed for such views. Nevertheless, Rempel notes several commonalities among the three Anabaptist theologians he studies. One is that they tended toward spiritualism, "that grace cannot be transmitted by material means." But this view was shaped by their belief that "the Christian life inseparably consisted of a relationship with God and with the church." Baptism was central for them as a covenant not only with Christ but with the church. And "the Lord's Supper was based not only on the memory of Christ's self-sacrifice but also on the communicants' pledge to imitate Christ in living with sister, brother, neighbor and enemy."

To restate this, Christ is not present in the material elements of Communion, the bread and wine, but in the church, the gathered body of Christ. And the focus in Communion is not just vertical (God and me) but horizontal (others and me).

At the same time, these theologians held together faith and Spirit. The Lord's Supper was not "a rational act of remembrance and a humanly willed remaking of covenant." Instead they understood faith "primarily as a gift of the Spirit."

When we look at Mennonites' celebration of Communion today, we find an evolution from its sixteenth-century origins. Traditional Mennonite celebration of Communion, Rempel writes, "is characterized . . . by an ethical earnestness." The celebration is infrequent (two to four times a year) and is preceded by a preparatory service of confession and reconciliation. But in the past generation this has changed. The preparatory service has largely disappeared; there is no longer an emphasis on reconciliation among believers.

"The common explanation for this change," Rempel writes, "is that the earlier ethical stringency had become graceless legalism." Communion has also become less somber and more celebratory of the body of Christ as the church. The earlier practice is now seen as too individualistic and funereal. Rempel sums up this change:

> The ethically binding horizontal dimension of the preparatory service . . . has been replaced by a vertical, devotional stress. On the other hand, the vertical orientation of the Communion proper has been replaced by a celebration of relationships among believers.

Rempel believes most Mennonites are unaware of the teachings of the Anabaptists and that other Christians can learn from them. For instance, he summarizes Pilgram Marpeck's view:

> The church's place in the event of communion is to gather in faith and love around bread and wine. The Spirit takes the elements and makes them co-witnesses with the Spirit. They then become the means of the church's union with Christ, of its participation in his body and blood.

And from Balthasar Hubmaier we understand

the Eucharist as gratitude which takes ethical form (as Christ gave himself for me, so I can give myself for others) and links worship to mission. This thrust contributes to a Christian self-understanding which is other-centered, translating faith into love and thanksgiving into sacrifice.

Combining the vertical and horizontal elements, Rempel concludes, "Anabaptism teaches that communion is the surpassing expression of reconciliation of Christians with God and with each other."

Many Mennonites (myself included) have felt a hunger for experiencing Christ's presence in the Eucharist and are drawn to dialogue with Catholics and others to explore this. We find the article on "The Lord's Supper" in *Confession of Faith in a Mennonite Perspective* too tepid when it describes Communion as "a sign by which the church thankfully remembers the new covenant which Jesus established by his death."

Marlene Kropf, a Mennonite teacher who has been involved in leadership of Bridgefolk, wrote an article in our magazine, "A Modest Proposal for Communion" (*The Mennonite*, Sept. 4, 2007), that calls for Communion to be joyful, nonviolent, just, open, and frequent. She concludes, "United at the Lord's Table and telling the story of Jesus' nonviolent love of friends and enemies, Christians may yet become grace-filled signs of God's love and mercy in a world longing for healing and hope."

This long excursus on Mennonite attitudes toward Communion raises questions about God's action and presence in the world, questions raised by prayer in its many forms. I will address this further in Chapter Eight.

Moving on, I've also referred to confession, both to one another when we've wronged someone and to God, acknowledging the ways we've failed to live as God has made us to live. This is simply being honest with God and with ourselves. Rolheiser calls this one of the "four nonnegotiable essentials to Christian spirituality." He says, "I am only healthy if there is an essential honesty in my life." Gandhi called truthtelling the root of peacemaking. Confession helps us live truthful lives. Corporate confession can serve as a helpful reminder and be a way to acknowledge corporate sins.

All prayer is a means of truthtelling, of living into the truth that we are created by God and live by God's breath. Delving deeper into prayer leads one to a surrender to silence. As Annie Dillard writes: "We are most deeply asleep at the switch when we fancy we control any switches at all. We sleep to time's hurdy-gurdy, we wake, if we ever wake, to the silence of God" (*Holy the Firm*).

Silence

Contemplative prayer is not part of Mennonite tradition, and silence is not a regular part of Mennonite worship. But if you watch a Mennonite build a cabinet, say, or another sew a quilt, you may witness a contemplative silence that is part of Mennonite spirituality.

Yet silence as prayer goes deeper. As Max Picard writes, "Silence . . . is not the mere absence of speech" but "a complete world in itself" (*The World of Silence*).

We live in a noisy society uncomfortable with silence. We are surrounded by noise wherever we go—the grocery store, the doctor's office, you name it, has music playing constantly. And many of us don't want to escape it; even if we're walking or running outside, we wear our iPods.

Silence unnerves us. Try implementing a period of silence in your church's worship. Even thirty seconds feels like an eternity.

Yet if we befriend it, silence may lead us deeper within ourselves and who knows where. I've been on silent retreats where even meals are eaten in silence. It feels weird the first day, but soon you get used to it and settle into it. Suddenly you notice things you would not have otherwise—the paintings on the wall, the sounds of the cooks in the kitchen or the birds outside your window, the people around you—because you are no longer distracted by your or others' speech. You use smiles or other expressions to communicate with others. And when you're alone, you move naturally toward prayer. Eventually the silence of God becomes less an absence than a fullness, a plenitude of peace.

Silence can lead us into a contemplation that invites us out of ourselves into God's presence. Maggie Ross writes that "the whole point of the journey into the fiery love of God is *self-forgetfulness*, a self-forgetfulness evolving from a self-awareness that gradually drops away as we become ever more found in the adoration of God in whom we find our true selves" (*The Fountain and the Furnace*).

Godric, the titular character of Frederick Buechner's wonderful novel, sums it up at the end of his life: "All's lost. All's found."

This is the great mystery of prayer and the theme of this book: We are found as we lose ourselves. And prayer helps us get lost, as it were.

At the beginning of this chapter I referred to the twin aspects of God that affect our prayer life—God's immanence and God's transcendence, what Ken Wilber calls descending and ascending. When we pray, we often picture or want a powerful doctor who will heal our ills. Or we want a mother who will hold us and comfort us in our trouble and never leave us. And God is both—and neither. Both describe God, but neither captures who God is. God is beyond us and beside us. God heals us and holds us. God "transcends and includes, brings forth and embraces, creates and loves, . . . unfolds and enfolds" (Ken Wilber, *A Brief History of Everything*).

Seeing God is what we long for. Augustine says, "Our entire task in this life consists in healing the eyes of the heart so that they may be able to see God."

Perfection

Be perfect, therefore, as your heavenly Father is perfect.
—Matthew 5:48

Thus he has given us, through these things, his precious and very great promises, so that through them you may escape from the corruption that is in the world because of lust, and may become participants of the divine nature.
—2 Peter 1:4

Perfection is neither more nor less than the soul's faithful cooperation with God.
—Jean-Pierre de Caussade, *Abandonment to Divine Providence*

Two disclaimers: (1) I didn't make "Perfection" Chapter Seven because seven is the perfect number, though it is a nice coincidence; (2) the subject of this chapter is perfection, not perfectionism.

I know the saying, "Nobody's perfect." But that's not in the Bible, whereas Matthew 5:48 (see above) is. Rather than write off this saying (and many others) about being perfect, I thought it worth exploring.

No one likes perfectionists, even those of us who are anal about many things, unless they are fixing our car or building our house. And even then, we get impatient when they take so long to do the job. When we hear the word *perfectionist*, we usually think of someone who is nitpicky, judgmental. And while that may match our image of God, I contend it shouldn't.

Mennonites have been accused of being perfectionists. When we mention pacifism, for example, others often say, That's well and good, but get real. The world's a bad place, and besides, nobody's perfect.

Individual Mennonites may be perfectionists, and Mennonites certainly have been judgmental, but as a group we are as imperfect as anyone, despite our ideals.

When we hear the word *perfect*, we often think of something flawless, correct in every detail. This fits at least one of Webster's definitions. We may describe the weather or a food item as perfect while we make an O with our thumb and forefinger and raise our remaining fingers as if showing the number 3.

I did a quick word study of *teleios*, the Greek word translated "perfect" in Matthew 5:48. Gerhard Kittel and Gerhard Friedrich's *Theological Dictionary of the New Testament* examines this word's use in Greek philosophy, where it can refer to full humanity, to right ethical choice or to someone who has all the virtues. In the Septuagint, the Greek Old Testament, they write, the word usually means unblemished, as in a lamb perfect for sacrificing. In the New Testament, the word means "undivided," "whole or complete," and occasionally "mature."

Jesus' sermon

With this background, let's look at Matthew 5:48, which marks the end of the first of three chapters in that Gospel that make up what's called the Sermon on the Mount. That so-called sermon, as I've pointed out, is a centerpiece for Mennonite teaching.

This verse comes at the culmination of a series of sayings of Jesus in which he compares his teaching with earlier teaching, using the phrase, "You have heard that it was said, . . . but I say to you." The last of these compares the command to "love your neighbor and hate your enemy" (the latter part—"hate your enemy"—is not found in the Old Testament or rabbinical teaching that's been preserved, though it likely represents popular understanding then and American policy now) with Jesus saying, "Love your enemies and pray for those who persecute you" (v. 44). This is how we show we are children of our Father in heaven.

And this is how we are to be perfect (teleios). Here that word could be translated "undivided." Just as God's love is not divided between neighbors and enemies, between the righteous and unrighteous, so our love is to be undivided. Children are to be like their parent.

Back when I was in Bible college, much of the teaching there followed a dispensationalist theology. This approach taught that God works with humanity differently in different dispensations. So you have innocent Adam and Eve, then the Fall, then God destroying the earth in a flood and making a covenant with Noah. Then comes the promise to Abraham, then the law given to Moses. Then God has Israel offer sacrifices as part of its worship. But after Jesus, sacrifices ended.

But what to do with Jesus' teachings? Since all that matters is being saved by the blood of Jesus and waiting for him to come again, those teachings can't apply to us now. That would be too much like "works righteousness," earning our salvation. But it's in the Bible, so we have to fit it in somewhere. Let's stick it in the next dispensation, the age to come, which means after Jesus comes back (the Second Coming).

This is all quite convenient. When Jesus says to love our enemies and be perfect, that doesn't apply to us. That's for a future age when all the sinners have been sent to hell (which begs the question of who these enemies are that we are to love). Being perfect is impossible anyway (as is loving one's enemies). Why would Jesus ask us (tell us really) to do the impossible?

One of my teachers at that school challenged the notion that God gives us commands we can't do, so we'll know we are sinners and get saved. He said, No, God gives a command that can be followed. We may find it difficult to obey because of our sinful tendencies, but it is not impossible. God doesn't play tricks with us.

When we hear, Be perfect, we automatically think, *That can't be right; we're all too fallible.* Then why, we have to ask, does Jesus give this command? (Notice I use present tense, assuming the view that Jesus' saying, while reported from the first century A.D., is addressed to us today who believe the Word of God is living and active. This, at least, is something Mennonites say they believe.) In saying this, is he not assuming it is doable? Or must we perform mental gymnastics, like the dispensationalists, and somehow get around it?

In his book *Beyond the Law*, Mennonite pastor Philip K. Clemens acknowledges the difficulty of this verse, that "if Jesus expects such an impossibility of us, then we know it's hopeless." But he wants to take the saying seriously, so he approaches it from a different perspective that is helpful, if not, well, perfect.

Clemens points out that Jesus is addressing a group, not an individual. The second-person pronouns (you's) in this passage are plural: "children of your [plural] Father" (v. 45), you [plural] are to be perfect "as your [plural] heavenly Father is perfect" (v. 48). "Jesus is describing the character of the community that lives beyond the law in the presence of God's goodness," Clemens writes.

This is a good corrective to American (and modern) individualism (see Chapter Four). We tend to read the you's in the Bible as singular when they are often plural. (This is a great handicap of the English language. Other languages distinguish singular and plural you.) Christians who read the Bible (not nearly enough do) often read it devotionally and ask, How does this verse or passage apply to me? That's not a bad question, but we neglect reading Scripture as a community and asking, How does this apply to us? That's something the early Anabaptists did but that few Mennonites in North America do, with some exceptions.

We practice that to some degree when we gather at conferences, either in regions or nationally. Often there is a scriptural focus and some discussion about what this means for us, but it doesn't go far, and its effectiveness is debatable. Another exception is in magazines like *The Mennonite*, for which I work. Articles appear that discuss certain teachings from the Bible. Sometimes those are discussed in the magazine via letters to the editor. More often, Sunday school classes discuss these articles as to how this should or should not apply to them. Such classes also discuss Scripture and how it applies. But where is the accountability? How seriously do such groups come to an agreement on how to respond?

Clemens goes on to clarify the meaning of "perfect." As I've already mentioned, and Clemens affirms, the Greek word translated "perfect" means "complete, whole, finished, full grown or fully developed." He writes, "We cannot make God's love complete or fully developed in us as separated individuals, just as one person cannot sing a congregational hymn."

Loving all

That's a good point, as far as it goes, but I don't think it meshes completely (perfectly?) with the logic of the text. Jesus describes God's love as perfect in that it includes everyone— neighbors and enemies, righteous and unrighteous. That, then, is how we are to be perfect—loving all.

Certainly that is no easy matter, for an individual or a group, but it fits with what the Bible emphasizes and what, dare I say, I've been emphasizing in this book as the heart of Mennonite spirituality. We are all—individuals and groups—created and called to love thoroughly and equally. This kind of love reflects the love that exists in the Triune God (the technical Greek word is *perichoresis*). It also reflects God's unconditional love toward the world, toward all people, all creation—giving, self-emptying.

In the Lukan parallel to this verse (from Jesus' sermon on the plain), Jesus says, "Be merciful, just as your Father is merciful" (Luke 6:36). Following the logic of these parallels, perfection means loving enemies, means being merciful.

Again, this is difficult to live out, and the more we mature, the better (we hope) we can live this way. And it's admittedly difficult sometimes to figure out how to love one's enemies or be merciful in a certain situation (that's where community discernment is helpful). But we're looking at a stance, a direction, a way of life we grow into. Another word for that kind of stance is Gelassenheit. We surrender ourselves to God's love and to what is in an attitude of love. And we do that best by living fully in each moment, aware of God's presence—in us and in the world.

I know this can sound esoteric, even amorphous. But living this way, practicing perfection, is, shall we say, visceral, day to day. It involves entering the mire of the world and the muck of our own selfish tendencies and seeking to surrender to God's love in concrete ways.

To approach this from another angle, let's look at what perfection is not. Back in my early years as a Christian, I made various attempts to live out this new faith perfectly. As do we all, I had my own notions of perfection. I thought of it more as not sinning. And sinning had less to do with not loving than with not adhering to my ideals.

I recall having failed to live up to my standards and determining to make a new start. June 1, 1970, was a Monday, and I decided that would make a good time to begin a new life of doing things right. I might have made it a few hours, I don't know. But soon I made a mistake—maybe I tripped over something, and I got angry, or I responded less than kindly to someone—and it ended. I tried to recover the first few times things went wrong. I knew God forgave, and I could move on, but after a while I grew frustrated and gave up on the enterprise. After all, one couldn't start a life of perfection on June 2.

I made other attempts and experienced more failure. Sometimes it involved masturbating and feeling guilty. Often it wasn't something I did but that events did not proceed as I wished. I wanted things to go smoothly, like in the movies (or at least in my imagination). Eating was another area of repeated failure. Being a good Christian, I decided, included eating healthy food. But every so often I'd give in and eat a Honey Bun (my weakness), and my foray into obedience and perfection was over.

The comment from Richard Rohr might have helped me, though it was written decades later: "The only true perfection available to us is the honest acceptance of our imperfection" (*Everything Belongs*). Or it may not have helped. I was young, immature. And remember, one meaning of teleios is "full-grown."

My problem—and the problem with our usual views—was that I viewed perfection as stasis, something neat and tidy, unchanging, when life just didn't work that way. Debbie Blue writes about how people—particularly religious people—talk about the need for stability: "stable homes, a stable environment for our children, stable personalities, stable marriages, stable jobs" (*From Stone to Living Word*). Christians often want—and want to provide—clear answers, simple solutions. But look around—at your life and the world. "Life isn't simple and coherent," Blue writes. "It is inexplicable and lush and desperate and sad and beautiful and scary."

A beautiful wildness

When we thank God for what is—a key to living in the present—we give thanks for a world teeming with life and variety and uncertainty, a beautiful wildness. As Blue writes, "It's outrageous to be alive."

Perfection, then, is lived out in the messiness of our lives and involves embracing that messiness in some strange, holy way.

In being called to perfection we are called to imitate what David Bentley Hart calls "the anarchic prodigality of [God's] love" (*The Beauty of the Infinite*). Such wild love is scandalous to ancient Greek (and modern) notions of perfection—clean, guarding against chaos, while God enters our world with all its dirty difference and embraces it in love. The story of God is one, Hart writes, in which "the being of creation is an essential peace, hospitable to all true difference, reflecting the infinite peace of God's triune life in its beauty and diversity."

Perfection, then, is not sameness, not some mechanical precision. The Triune God includes difference—Father, Son, Holy

Spirit—and God's creation certainly teems with variety, a complex beauty scientists continue to explore and find mystifying.

Creation—in its wild complexity—God says, is "very good" (Gen. 1:31). And humanity is created in God's image (Gen. 1:27). This becomes a basis for the perfection—the beauty, as Eastern Orthodoxy emphasizes—God is drawing us into. Yet these truths bump up against the concepts of fallenness and original sin. We are, according to this way of thinking, tainted by sin, affected intrinsically by what Adam and Eve did back in the garden. Just look around, say those emphasizing these beliefs, at the evil in the world. It's obvious humanity is fallen.

How we put these beliefs together is beyond the boundaries of this book and beyond my powers of thought. Better minds have grappled with them. But Mennonite spirituality keeps returning to Jesus, and in this chapter we turn to his command to "be perfect." Mennonites want to take Jesus seriously and put into practice what he says. And a premise of that approach is that, if we are tainted, it is not to the extent that we cannot do what Jesus commands. Otherwise, why command it?

Deification

This topic can also lead us into an area that is not an aspect of Mennonite spirituality but perhaps might enrich it: deification. I know, it sounds like heresy, even blasphemy; we can't become God. But it relates to that curious verse in 2 Peter (1:4) about becoming "participants of the divine nature." What does that mean? Since it's in the Bible (the New Testament, no less), we must take it seriously, yes?

My interest in this stems partly from my exposure to Eastern Orthodoxy. One of my college friends, Warren Farha, grew up Orthodox and returned to it fully after a foray into evangelicalism during college. Over the years, he has introduced me to various books (he owns a bookstore), and I've worshiped at his church at various times, particularly the Pascha service on Easter eve, which is a powerful experience.

As I've learned about Orthodoxy, I've noted some parallels with Mennonite spirituality. There is the sometimes awkward parallel of ethnic identity tied closely with church membership. My friend Warren and many of the members of his church are of Lebanese descent, for example. Another parallel is the emphasis on embodiment, which I will explore more in Chapter Eight.

Then there's the matter of original sin and the Fall that I mentioned earlier. Orthodoxy, as Timothy Ware writes in *The Orthodox Church*, holds "a less exalted idea of man's [sic] state before he fell [and] is also less severe than the west in its view of the consequences of the Fall." Augustine, a huge influence on theology in the West (Catholic and Protestant), taught that Adam was perfect, then fell into corruption. Orthodoxy, following Irenaeus, says Adam's perfection was potential.

Thus, writes Ware, "the image of God is distorted by sin but never destroyed." Contrary to the Calvinist notion of "the depravity of man," Orthodoxy retains the belief that humans have free will, dependent as it is on God's grace. Orthodoxy describes this relationship between God's grace and human freedom as synergy.

Mennonites don't have a developed theological tradition, so it's difficult to compare them with Orthodoxy. Nevertheless, Mennonites retain a belief (in their gut if not in their books) in human freedom. And they tend to agree with Orthodoxy that infants are innocent and not tainted by guilt—and therefore need not be baptized to avoid either hell or purgatory.

Let's move on—or back—to the subject of deification. This is a dominant theme in Orthodoxy and in the Church Fathers. (For example, Irenaeus of Lyons in the second century said that God "became what we are to make us what he is," and Athanasios of Alexandria in the fourth century said that "God became man in order that we may become gods.") Yet we in the West hear nothing about it. Or if we do, we usually discount it out of hand. I want to explore it because I think it may relate to this subject of perfection.

Ware offers a helpful outline of its meaning in six points:

Deification is not something reserved for a few select initiates but something intended for all alike.

The fact that a man [sic] is being deified does not mean that he ceases to be conscious of sin.

There is nothing esoteric or extraordinary about the methods we must follow to be deified.

Deification is not a solitary but a 'social' process.

Love of God and of other men [sic] must be practical: Orthodoxy rejects all forms of Quietism, all types of love which do not issue in action.

Deification presupposes life in the Church, life in the sacraments.

Ware expands on each of these points, but I want to note the similarity of most of these to what we've been describing as Mennonite spirituality (in its prescriptive or ideal, not always its descriptive or real form). Mennonites uphold what they call the priesthood of all believers—the notion that all have access to God. They retain a consciousness of sin, which goes right along with notions of humility. I've tried all along to say this stuff isn't esoteric; it's not a Gnostic sect where you need some secret knowledge. (For the "social" emphasis, see Chapter Four. For "practical," see Chapter One.)

Then we get to number six. Mennonites certainly emphasize life in the church, but that has a whole different meaning from what Ware means. Mennonites don't believe they are the true church, though they may act like they do. And I've already noted the lack of emphasis among Mennonites on sacramentality.

Orthodoxy addresses the two main objections to deification (also called divinization or theosis). One is that only God is divine and humans can't be. In the fourteenth century, Gregory Palamas distinguished the "energies" of God, which we can know, from the "essence" of God, which we cannot know. This distinction between God's energies and essence, Ware points out, goes back to the fourth-century Cappadocian Fathers (Gregory of Nazianzus, Basil the Great and Gregory of Nyssa).

The other chief objection is the idea of perfection itself as some defined state. In his book *The Orthodox Way*, Ware says in his prologue that the Christian life, according to Orthodoxy, is a journey. "To be a Christian is to be a traveler," he writes. Deification, then, is not a state of perfection but a way of life that partakes in God's energies.

Also opposing the idea of what he calls "divinization" being some state of perfection is Richard Valantasis, an Episcopal priest who grew up Orthodox, in his book *Centuries of Holiness*. He writes that divinization will look different for each person and community. "Divinization," he writes, "says that all difference will ultimately be shown to have the same divine nature and process as every other divergent and diverse being."

Valantasis notes that divinization is not naïve, does not claim that everything is already divinized. Rather, "much of one's life, social relations and relationships to the larger cosmos are marked by a suppression of the divine energy and by a repression of the divine impulse." He, too, emphasizes that it is a journey, a process.

I realize this talk of divine energy sounds New Age-ish, even though it goes back to the fourth century. But think of it as the Holy Spirit infusing our lives as we offer them to God, giving us the strength (the energy) to love as God loves—perfectly.

Various traditions have emphasized perfection. Methodists, for example, teach sanctification in this life leading to a "perfect best" in the fullness of time. Pentecostals have taught the baptism of the Holy Spirit as a "second blessing." Others, including Mennonites, have more often looked down on such teachings, when they've looked at all from their more insular church life.

While these traditions may tie such blessing or sanctification to certain dramatic experiences, at their root is a surrender to God that is similar to Gelassenheit. Mennonite spirituality, however, would perhaps emphasize more the daily, mundane surrender to God, while also seeing that manifesting itself primarily in the church, the gathered body of Christ. And I would contend that Mennonites, if they move toward perfection or

Gelassenheit at all, will tend to do so on their own steam, gritting their teeth and doing what's right.

But the vast majority of Mennonites do not view the Christian life—following Jesus—in terms of perfection. It's just not on their radar.

I want to put it there, for any who might look—and listen.

Let's recount, then, the points I've tried to make in this chapter:

Jesus calls us to imitate God's perfection by being perfect (Matt. 5:48).

Perfection, according to the context of that verse, refers to a complete love that includes neighbor and enemy.

We, the community, are primarily called to be perfect. But "we" includes us as individuals.

Perfection is not a mechanistic, legalistic state but a dynamic, visceral, moment-by-moment process.

Orthodoxy teaches deification, which stems from the biblical notion of participating in the divine nature (2 Pet. 1:4).

We can know and experience God's energies, though not God's essence.

(There must be seven, right?) At the root of perfection is the Mennonite notion of Gelassenheit, surrender to God in each moment.

Because we often fail (though not because we are bound to fail) to surrender and receive God's energies, we depend upon forgiveness and grace. That, in fact, is the divine air we breathe. We cannot live without that grace. Our task (and Mennonites love tasks) is to live in the reality of that dependence, to grow in our awareness of that Reality.

A story of perfect love

Let me close with an example of what such surrender, and such perfect love, can look like. I hesitate to offer it because it is so dramatic, when most of our ways of living out such perfection will be mundane, such as giving in to our spouse or showing kindness to a stranger.

In September 2008, I attended meetings of the Executive Board of Mennonite Church USA as part of my job, to report on them for the magazine. One evening we met with leaders from several Mennonite congregations in Philadelphia. Someone asked Tuyen Nguyen, pastor of the local Vietnamese Mennonite Church, to tell about an experience he had some fifteen years earlier, when he wasn't a pastor but a member of that congregation.

During a Sunday worship service, he said, a man ran into the building, chased by another man, who carried a gun. Tuyen saw that the man being chased could not escape, so he stepped between him and the man with the gun. He did this without much thought, but his action grew out of his understanding that Jesus absorbed the violence of others in his own body, and we are to do the same.

The man with the gun stopped and pointed the gun at Nuyen a moment, then turned and left. Later he came back and talked to Nuyen. Some months later he gave his life to Christ, was baptized, and joined the congregation. The man he had chased that day was his father.

Tuyen told us, "We can be peaceful because God is in control." By control, it was clear, he did not mean that God controlled every movement each person made. Each actor was free to act as he chose—the chaser, the chasee, and Tuyen, who chose to stand between them. He meant that we are not in control; God is in charge, and we do not have to make things come out right. We are instead to surrender ourselves to God's Spirit and in the way Jesus taught.

Again, this is a dramatic example of perfection, overcoming fear, and loving neighbor and enemy. But Tuyen, I imagine, was already practicing this in other, more mundane ways each day.

We can practice patience, be peaceful—as individuals and as communities—ceding any results of our actions, prayerfully loving in the complete, merciful manner of God's perfect love. We can do all this because of God's loving presence, which is our next—and final—destination.

Chapter Eight

Presence

We cannot attain the presence of God because we're already totally in the presence of God. What's absent is awareness.
—Richard Rohr, *Everything Belongs*

Kadosh, kadosh, kadosh, Adonai tsera'ot,
Melo khol ha'arets kevodo.
(Holy, holy, holy, the Lord of Hosts,
His presence fills all the earth.)
—Jewish prayer in synagogue

If we take eternity to mean not infinite temporal duration but timelessness, eternal life belongs to those who live in the present.
—Ludwig Wittgenstein

We come to the end, and "in our end is our beginning," as T. S. Eliot memorably wrote ("The Four Quartets"). If spirituality, as I observed in the Preface, is living in the Spirit, then our living, everything at all, has to do with the presence of God. Living, as well, has to do with how we are present—and how we recognize that Presence. Our living, from beginning to end, is in God's presence, and our goal, as it were, is to be aware of that.

God's presence is another of the great mysteries of our faith. We believe God is omnipresent (everywhere at all times), yet in our prayers we often ask God to be present. What we're really doing in such prayers is expressing our desire that we be aware of God's presence. We also talk about God's presence in Communion, however we think about that. Such talk implies God's absence outside that holy meal, which goes against our belief in God's omnipresence.

This raises the question, Does God need to change, or do we? I'll guess you know the answer.

A major preoccupation of Christian spirituality through the ages is how to experience God's presence. In his monumental history of Western Christian mysticism, *The Presence of God*, Bernard McGinn writes that "the mystical element of Christianity is that part of its belief and practices that concerns the preparation for, the consciousness of and the reaction to what can be described as the immediate or direct presence of God" (*Volume I: The Foundations of Mysticism*).

Whoa, you may be saying. I'm not a mystic and don't want to be. Fair enough. But we can learn from mystics. After all, mystics tend to get to the heart of the matter and take the basics more seriously than the rest of us. We want to grow in our awareness of God's presence and our experience of that presence, right? (If wrong, you may stop reading. If you're not sure but are curious, read on.) That's what the Christian mystical tradition is about.

Christian mystics over the centuries have developed ways of growing in such awareness. These ways grew out of their understanding in their context. While we have much to learn from them, we also must learn to grow out of our own understanding and in our context.

Part of that context may be that we hold down a job and have a family and cannot spend hours per day in meditation or contemplative prayer. An aspect of Gelassenheit, which I've stressed as a root element of Mennonite spirituality, is accepting what is. This doesn't mean we don't work for change in ourselves or our world. It does mean we live out of our context, the time and place in which we live, rather than pretend or wish we were elsewhere.

Out of that context—and you know your own—how do we grow in our awareness of God's presence?

How is God present?

A first step is to understand more fully what the presence of God means. With the caveat that we can never understand fully (only more fully) what it means, let's start with how the word is used in the Bible.

Well, there isn't just one word translated "presence," but one common term in the Greek Bible is *parousia*, which refers to an active presence and is often translated "coming," as in Jesus' Second Coming. It's used in the secular world for the visits of rulers or high officials. The Old Testament uses it to refer to God's coming in various ways (dreams, theophanies, storms, visions, the quiet breath, God's Word or Spirit), in history, as world king and the coming of the Messiah.

In the New Testament, parousia is used not for Jesus' initial coming but for his "coming in glory." Jesus sees it as both imminent and requiring perseverance. And "he attempts no date setting and divests the *parousia* of its political element, stressing the ethical aspect (Matt. 25:14ff.)" (*Theological Dictionary of the New Testament*).

This all gets complex theologically. We wait in hope for Jesus' coming (presence), but isn't Jesus already present through the Spirit?

Yes and yes. We wait for a coming that will be more concrete and complete—the perfection we grow toward, the "perfect best," as the Methodists say. Yet God is present through the Spirit. Remember the resurrected Jesus breathing on his followers and saying, "Receive the Holy Spirit" (John 20:22). That Presence leads to concrete actions of forgiveness, proclaiming good news, healing, coming together as a community and sharing possessions, including people outside the Jewish community, standing up fearlessly to the rulers. The Spirit's presence leads us on the path of perfection, away from fear toward love, away from ourselves toward others in acts of self-giving, thus imitating God, whose Self-giving was starkly evident in Jesus' torture and death.

This may sound laudatory and heroic and therefore outside our ken. But these early followers of Jesus were fallible humans—the Bible records many of their mistakes, misunderstandings and myopia—who grew, step by step, into a greater awareness of God's presence in their lives—and, more importantly, their life together. Each moment they had choices about how to respond. The Book of Acts, for example, tends to record the good choices of those who became leaders of the fledgling movement, though it also records Ananias and Sapphira (Acts 5) and the contentious Jerusalem Council (Acts 15). Nevertheless, the church grew because many people made decisions and acted in response to an awareness of God's presence. Likely they would have conceived that presence as in their community, not in themselves. Likely we tend to conceive it more the other way around. I believe both are true and have important implications.

While these early followers may have had a sense of Jesus' coming (*parousia*) to mark the end of the ages, they acted in their present, as we are to act in ours.

Our experience

How then do we experience God's presence? We acknowledge from Scripture that God is everywhere, that, as Jews pray, "God's presence fills all the earth." But is this comforting or disconcerting? The Psalmist seems troubled by it: "Where can I go from your spirit? Or where can I flee from your presence?" (Psalm 139:7). It depends on how we imagine God. Is God for us a stern judge, frowning on every misstep we make? Or is God a bemused old man who largely ignores us? Some seem to portray God as an eager servant who does our bidding.

We may imagine God differently at different times, in different circumstances. Often we feel that God is elusive. We experience what's called in Latin *Deus absconditus*, the hidden God. We may often, like Isaiah, want God to "tear open the heavens and come down" (64:1). But that "parousia" does not happen. Instead we wait.

Let's ask a prior question: How do we experience the loving presence of another, since we believe that God is love? Our first loving presence is likely our mother. While I do not consider my late mother especially affectionate, I have a fond memory of lying in the back seat of our '57 Pontiac on trips across country as a child, my head in her lap.

I also recall the terror of absence. One afternoon, my mother drove to my elementary school and left me in the car while she went inside to meet with my teacher during parent-teacher conferences. (This was the early 1960s in small-town mid-America.) She was away much longer than the usual ten to fifteen minutes, and I grew more and more anxious. After a while I was certain she had been murdered, and I'd be left alone.

When she emerged from the building and walked across the parking lot, I frantically wiped away my tears. But when she got in the car, she noticed and asked, in her knowing way, "What's wrong? Were you worried?" I nodded, swallowed a sob. She explained that the parent ahead of her took a long time, that there was nothing to worry about.

Nothing to worry about. Sounds like Jesus: "Do not worry about your life" (Matt. 6:25). "Why are you afraid?" (Mark 4:40). "Do not be afraid, little flock" (Luke 12:32). The most frequent command in the Bible is (in some form), Do not fear. It occurs more than 120 times. But that doesn't stop us.

We live in an atmosphere of fear. Our government tells us to fear terrorists, at times even color-coding the danger level. According to surveys, the greatest fear of American adults is speaking in public. What about teenagers? You may think it's fear of death, but that's not even in the top forty. Their greatest fear is to lose their parents, either through death or divorce. (Like me as a child in that car.)

The remedy to fear, says the Bible, is love: "Perfect love casts out fear" (1 John 4:18). We've already looked at God's perfect love (Chapter Seven) and how we are to imitate it. The presence of such perfect love relieves our fear, our anxiety.

When the IRS flagged New Creation Fellowship back in 1980 and called Jeanne and me in to ask us about our tax return, we were anxious. Because we were part of a common treasury, all our income went into it. Tax laws only allowed us to claim up to half our earnings as contributions, which we did. The IRS agent asked us questions about "this New Creation Fellowship," and we felt conflicted because we didn't want our answers to affect others, so we said little. He scheduled another meeting; he wasn't going to let this go.

When we told NCF's pastors (we called them elders) what happened, they apologized for sending us into that situation alone. They went to the next meeting with the IRS agent. Their presence in our stead felt loving and relieved my anxiety—at least for a while. We eventually lost thousands of dollars because of the IRS ruling, and the common treasury later folded. Nevertheless, those pastors served as our presence, our advocate (a translation of the word Jesus uses to describe the Holy Spirit in John 14:16).

We've all been in situations that seemed easier, less anxious, because someone was with us who cared for us. They weren't just with us "in spirit" but by their bodily presence.

This is what we often long for from God. We may believe God is with us, but we want that Presence embodied. And such a desire is not heretical, because the God we worship has come "in the flesh."

Embodied presence

The incarnation (which means "in the flesh") is one of the central doctrines of Christianity—and one that distinguishes it from other religions. This doctrine, writes Richard Valantasis, "focuses attention on the simultaneous humiliation of God descending into human existence and the exaltation of humanity being made worthy to bear God."

The early church argued long and hard against Gnostics to insist that Jesus was fully human and fully divine. This has huge implications for us who are baptized into Christ's body. We then become capable of expressing the divine life within us. As Valantasis puts it, "Christ was divine and took on the human body, the Christian is embodied and takes on the divine life."

This takes us back to my earlier point (in the Preface) that "spiritual" does not mean noncorporeal or disembodied. In our spirituality we are to follow the Spirit's leading and manifest the divine life in the arena of worldly existence.

A further implication of the incarnation (and of the Creation) is that the world is "the place where God may be seen and known," writes Valantasis. Further,

> everything in the world—every religious tradition, every scientific exploration, every medical breakthrough, every political situation, the environment, outer space—everything in the world has been altered by the presence of God in the physical universe.

This means that when we treat the world as evil or God's creation as something to be squandered or misused, we are being heretical, adopting a Gnostic disdain for the evil flesh, which many considered a "prisonhouse for the soul." Our spirituality, then, is to be embodied and to embrace the world, which "is not neutral and is not evil but central and groaning to manifest the presence of the divine," writes Valantasis.

God's presence is embodied in the world in many, various ways. We may experience this presence through the natural world, through the arts, through the love of others or thousands of other means. Scripture points to certain practices, such as Communion, that make God's presence more real, more palpable, to us. Jesus' parable of the judgment of the nations (Matt. 25:31-46) points to his presence in those in need: the hungry, the thirsty, the stranger, the naked, the sick, the prisoner.

Even those outside any religious tradition have "a longing for Transcendence," as Sandra M. Levy writes in *Imagination and the Journey of Faith*. She describes this as a longing for release from the mundane, a longing to transcend our own finite limits of mortality, a longing to meet God or the transcendent Other beneath and beyond the ordinary of our everyday lives.

We all share this longing, this gut-level intuition of God's hovering presence, and we look for ways to make that more real. To do so we use our imagination. Our Christian tradition provides many ways to do this. When we take part in Communion, for example, we taste bread and drink from the cup as a way to experience the real presence of Christ.

As I wrote in Chapter Six, Mennonites have not emphasized Communion, or the Eucharist, as the "real presence" of Christ in the way other traditions have, though interest in it is burgeoning. And I'm not qualified (and you may not be interested) to delineate the various understandings of the Eucharist. I still hold to what I wrote in an editorial in the February 28, 1995, issue of *The Mennonite*: "When we celebrate Communion we take part in a mystery. It is an act that cannot be fully explained but one that carries deep significance for Christians."

Robert Webber places this in a larger context: "The presence of Christ at bread and wine is a mystery situated in the larger mystery of the entire story of God's relationship to the world" (*Ancient-Future Worship*).

Imagination

Ignatian spirituality encourages the use of the imagination through "praying the Scriptures." To simplify, this involves reading a passage from the Bible, usually a narrative, and imagining oneself in that scene. For example, say you choose the story of Jesus healing a paralytic (Mark 2:1-12). In this practice you read the story several times, then imagine yourself in it. You involve your senses by imagining what you see, hear, smell, feel, taste. You may place yourself in the role of one or more characters in the story, or you may place yourself there and see what happens. What does Jesus say to you? How do you reply? It can be revealing, even healing.

Speaking of which, you can also invite Jesus' presence in parts of your own story or life experience, as in theophostic prayer (see Chapter Six). In the late 1970s, while a member of NCF, our leaders learned a practice called "resting in the Spirit." To explain it, let me describe my experience of it.

One afternoon I met with my pastor and two others I trusted. I stood in front of a mattress and prayed while the others prayed for me. Soon I felt myself relax and fell back. My friends caught me and eased me down onto the mattress. I then opened my imagination to whatever might come. The idea, as I recall, is that one often recalled (or imagined) one's birth. This happened with me. I saw myself as a baby in the nursery. People were looking at me through a window. I wanted someone to pick me up and hold me, but no one did. I then resigned myself to this situation.

One goal of such an exercise is to learn what "faith judgments" one has made. Mine was that my needs aren't going to be met, so I may as well resign myself to this and get by on my own.

I realized that this kind of stoic sense of resignation and self-reliance described at least in part my general stance toward life. And while this had its helpful aspects and helped me get by, it basically denied the active presence of God in my life.

The next step in this prayer exercise was to invite Jesus to come to me in that scene in my imagination. And that's what happened. I imagined Jesus coming to me as a baby and picking me up, then holding me and comforting me. Was this figure the bathrobe and sandals picture often presented in children's Bibles? No, but that didn't really matter. I felt loved in that moment. And, you may imagine, my friends were in tears as I described for them my experience.

At another time I prayed with someone who "rested in the Spirit," and I was moved to tears. That person's experience was not the same as mine, but the effect was similar. Both of us gained an insight into how we approached life and experienced a sense of healing as we imagined God's loving presence through this form of prayer.

The ensuing lesson for me, then, was (and is) to imagine God's presence with me in each moment, but particularly when I face a situation in which I tend to revert to my faith judgment of stoic resignation and self-reliance. I've learned—and continue to learn—to respond to situations by letting myself feel whatever emotion presents itself, perhaps grieve a loss or cry at a hurt, then reaching out to others for support, all the while believing God is hurting with me and is present and embodied through those friends I reach out to for support.

You can imagine this is not easy. Although I've not been in one, I'd guess that Twelve-Step groups operate on a similar basis, without bringing Jesus into the equation.

Another element of the Christian (mostly Orthodox) tradition that I've found helpful in making God's presence more real is the use of icons. In his book *Praying With Icons*, Jim Forest writes, "One of the most important roles played by icons in Christian history has been to proclaim the physical reality of Jesus Christ, God incarnate."

Icons reflect this reality by showing that Jesus had, and has, a face, a body. And so do Mary and the many other saints portrayed in iconography. Icons, Forest writes, are "windows of connection" that aid our awareness "that we live in the presence of God and amid a 'cloud of witnesses.'"

Icons are not idols, not ends in themselves, but means of seeing, connecting with God in our prayers. We look not at the icons but through them to see the face of Christ.

One of my favorite icons—and one I use in my prayer times each day—is the Encaustic Icon of Jesus from Saint Catherine's Monastery in Sinai. It is the oldest surviving icon, dating to the sixth century. Thomas Cahill even thinks its image "may go back to the first century and even be based on eyewitness accounts." But that's not why I'm drawn to it, or even because it shows Jesus holding a book. I'm drawn to the eyes, one gentle and one more serious. The eyes seem to look straight at me. And gazing at Jesus' gaze through this icon, I feel his presence, his kind and harsh love, a love that knows me thoroughly and embraces me fully.

I've noted the centrality of the incarnation for Christian faith, and it's all the more important to emphasize in our current religious culture, especially in the West, which tends to treat God as an idea and spirituality as a bodiless practice of conceiving God for one's personal well-being. But, Forest writes, "God is not an idea, and praying is not an exercise to improve our concept of God. Prayer is the cultivation of the awareness of God's actual presence." And the heart of spirituality, Mennonite or otherwise, as the mystics, church fathers and mothers, and particularly the Bible make clear, is love.

Love

Love in Scripture is not merely a feeling and certainly not an idea. It is tied to action. God is love because God showed love in saving us, rescuing us from our waywardness. And we are called to imitate God by loving others—both neighbors and enemies. "It is through the protective care for creation, especially care for each other," Forest writes, "that we most clearly manifest our love of God."

The Bible reflects an empirical bias. Though not visible, God is manifested through deeds in the physical world. John the Baptist wanted a word of confirmation that Jesus was the long-awaited Messiah. Jesus told the messengers, "Go and tell John what you have seen and heard: the blind receive their sight, the lame walk, the lepers are cleansed, the deaf hear, the dead are raised, the poor have good news brought to them" (Luke 7:22).

When Philip wanted to convince Nathanael to follow Jesus with him, he said, "Come and see" (John 1:46). Even when Jesus is resurrected, he is presented not as some ethereal presence but as a body with the marks of his torture and death.

If we believe that "the Word became flesh and lived among us" (John 1:14), we must resist the notion that flesh is evil. Each time we divide ourselves into body and mind, or body and spirit, we distort the way God created us, as unified beings.

Our spirituality must be embodied to be real. We live as bodies, and all that we do is to be in obedience to the Spirit.

Thus, dishwashing, house-building, changing diapers, or haul-ing trash are to be spiritual activities every bit as much as pray-ing, preaching, or singing hymns.

Jesus was unembarrassed by the body. He not only touched lepers and mingled with other outcasts, he let himself be touched and cared for—for example, by the woman suffering from hemorrhages for twelve years (Luke 8:43) and the woman who bathed his feet with her tears and dried them with her hair (Luke 7:38). He scandalized not only the religious leaders but his own followers. We, too, if we are honest, are likely scandal-ized by such actions.

Part of the genius of Mennonite spirituality is in recaptur-ing the early church's insistence on our faith being lived out in the real world. Knowing Christ requires following him in life.

For Anabaptist martyrs, carrying Christ's cross was not an idea but something they actually suffered in their bodies. Also they saw their faith as having a direct impact on their posses-sions and how those are shared.

Mennonites today retain a sense of embodied faith. We are drawn to doing service with our hands. We are drawn to food, to making quilts or putting together school kits for needy chil-dren overseas. Many have been drawn to healing professions such as medicine or nursing. Others are involved in trades, in business.

Another emphasis of Mennonite spirituality (see Chapter Four) is on community. As Stephanie Paulsell points out in her book *Honoring the Body: Meditations on a Christian Practice,*

> The integrity of our bodies is a gift from God, but the meaning of our bodies does not stop at the boundaries of our skin. For we belong to one another, and so we are called to attend to the effects of our choices.

God is present in the physical—in creation, in the poor, even in the face of our enemy—and we grow in love as we grow in awareness of this mystery. Awareness is all, as Thomas Mer-ton said to his fellow monks a few years before his death:

Life is this simple: We are living in a world that is absolutely transparent, and God is shining through it all
the time. This is not just a fable or a nice story. It is true.
If we abandon ourselves to God and forget ourselves, we
see it sometimes, and we see it maybe frequently. God
manifests himself everywhere, in everything, in people
and in things and in nature and in events. It becomes
very obvious that he is everywhere and in everything and
we cannot be without him. You cannot be without God.
It's impossible. It's simply impossible. (Quoted in *Praying With Icons*)

Simple, yes, but it takes a lifetime of practice to see this reality and live in it.

And seeing this reality of God's presence helps us then reflect God's presence to others. Henri Nouwen writes,

God loves the people of the world so much that we were
chosen to become the vehicle for God's self-revelation.
Sinful men and women made of dust, not pure, immate-
rial angels, were chosen to share the mystery of God's
inner life, expressed in Father, Son and Spirit. (*Behold the
Beauty of the Lord*)

Ministry of presence

Mennonites have tended toward such a "ministry of presence" more than many Christian groups. For example (there are
many), Mennonites began Mennonite Central Committee in
the 1920s to help refugees fleeing persecution and starvation in
Russia. Out of this organized aid to their own grew a ministry of
development in which volunteers go live in places of need
around the world for three years or more at a time. While they
go "in the name of Christ" (a slogan of MCC), they do not go to
proselytize or begin churches. They help with community development through agricultural work, teaching, social work,
and organizing. Today, this work is usually done in cooperation
with local groups doing similar work. MCC provides bodies, re-

sources, and expertise when needed, while the local organizations call the shots.

Thus, while these Mennonites are doing stuff (how could they exist otherwise, being Mennonites), a major aspect of their mission is simply being there, being present with these communities and letting their supporters in North America know what's going on.

Civilian Public Service began as an alternative to military service during World War II. This had a dynamic effect on Mennonite churches. While it developed out of Mennonites' pacifism and refusal to fight in the war, it led to many ministries of presence. For example, some CPS workers were assigned to mental health institutions, most of which in the 1940s had deplorable conditions. Inmates (a more fitting term than patients) at times were left to roam the halls, sometimes naked, unclean amid their waste, some chained to walls.

After the war, some CPS workers wanted change and later formed several Mennonite mental health centers. These helped revolutionize the field as they developed more humane ways to treat patients.

Other Mennonites began prison ministries. Others moved to inner cities. All the while, Mennonites, like other Christian groups, were sending missionaries overseas. Many of these ministries included and were motivated by the desire to spread "the saving message of Jesus Christ." But a recurring element of many of these ministries was the need to be with people where they lived—in prison, in an inner city, in Congo or India or Colombia.

The motivation for such ministries was complex and likely included love for God and love for others as well as wanting others to believe as they do or needing to accomplish something to feel fulfilled. But their being present with others often changed them as well, a symbiosis of presence that reflects God's presence among us.

Ministries of presence have political effects, too. Christian Peacemaker Teams, begun in 1987 by Mennonites and

Brethren, defines itself with the slogan "Getting in the Way." CPT workers go to areas of conflict and seek to get in the way, form a kind of buffer between groups engaged in violent (or potentially violent) behavior. They try to bring understanding between groups while also informing their supporters in North America (and elsewhere by now) of injustices, encouraging them at times to contact their government officials, since the policies of national governments often exacerbate conflict in various communities.

"Getting in the Way" also refers to the way of Jesus, following Jesus on the road that may lead to the cross. Thus, CPT contends that Christians should be willing to give their lives in the cause of peace, just as soldiers give their lives in the cause of war.

To date, two CPT workers have died during their service. George Weber, seventy-three, died in Iraq as a result of a car accident on Jan. 6, 2003. Tom Fox, fifty-five, was kidnapped in Iraq with three other CPT workers on November 26, 2005. They were held 118 days. Fox was killed on March 9, 2006, while the others—Jim Loney, Norman Kember, and Harmeet Singh Sooden—were rescued by British forces on March 23. (See *In Harm's Way* by Kathleen Kern.)

CPT's central purpose, as stated in its guiding principles, is "to glorify the Prince of Peace." Despite its more public nature of serving in hot spots, much of CPT's work, its attempt to glorify the Prince of Peace, happens in fairly mundane ways. As Kathleen Kern writes,

> For every encounter in which CPT volunteers have been at the right place at the right time to prevent violence, they have spent hundreds of hours drinking tea on routine visits to families more interested in talking about the small details of their lives than theory and practice of nonviolence. They have spent hundreds of hours documenting violence that happened before CPT could prevent it, hundreds of hours planning nonviolent strategies and public witnesses that in the end bore little fruit.

She notes that "while many CPTers do have extraordinary abilities, most accomplish what they do simply by following the extraordinary example of Jesus Christ, who nonviolently got in the way of systems that dealt in death and exploitation." And while the work may look heroic on paper, Kern writes, "most CPTers would sheepishly admit that most of the conflict-resolution skills they learn in training are practiced largely within the teams." However, she adds, "managing conflict well within a team is no small thing."

Thus, CPT represents Mennonite spirituality in many ways. It practices not only peace but community (politics) and patience. Often CPT volunteers also exhibit the other chapter titles of this book: play (yes, play), prayer, the perfection of loving enemies as well as neighbors and, notably, presence.

In February 1995, I was part of a group (with three Canadian journalists) that traveled in the West Bank under the guidance of MCC "country representative" John Lapp. One of our stops was Hebron, where CPT workers Kathleen Kern and Wendy Lehman were exploring beginning a CPT work.

My first impression of them was their friendliness and humor. I'd been active in various peace groups over the years, and too many of them seemed dour and took themselves too seriously. Kathleen and Wendy were not jovial—neither of them extroverts—but seemed at ease and—here's the key phrase—unhurried. They certainly understood the gravity of the conflict going on in Hebron and how difficult it would be to try to address it. One year earlier to the day we were there, a settler named Goldstein had entered the local mosque (ostensibly the burial place of the biblical Abraham and Sarah) and killed twenty-nine worshipers with a gun. Others eventually beat him to death. (We visited a memorial at the nearby Jewish settlement that honored him as a martyr.)

These women also knew their movements were limited by their being women. Yet they seemed undeterred. They exhibited a mixture of humility and doggedness, which are appropriate adjectives for Mennonite spirituality.

The Hebron CPT work did begin and continued until the fall of 2008. Many CPTers spent time there and took part in various activities, most of them mundane yet some dramatic. (See Kern's account of a demonstration there on Jan. 10, 1999, in the Prologue to *In Harm's Way*.)

CPT certainly employs strategy when it can, but much of the time their workers are ad libbing, adjusting to the realities on the ground. As Indiana Jones says in *Raiders of the Lost Ark*, "I'm making this up as I go along." One of CPT's guiding principles includes "a clear recognition of our dependency on God's Spirit for security and leading."

An important part of each team's day, Kathleen and Wendy told me, is praying together. CPT, like the Benedictines, emphasizes prayer and work, though the groups live that out differently.

While CPT's presence demonstrates some of what Mennonite spirituality is about, so also does a family in rural Indiana caring for one another, its members active in their congregation, tending their garden, welcoming their neighbors and other guests at their table, where they pray together and laugh about each other's foibles. So, too, does the young Mennonite professional working faithfully at his job in Seattle, or the small business owner in eastern Pennsylvania looking for ways to expand her business, treat her employees well, and perhaps hire more.

These and many others try to "follow Jesus" as best they can, seeking the encouragement of others trying to do the same, worshiping together. In these ways they seek to experience God's presence and demonstrate God's presence in the way they treat those around them, particularly those who hunger and thirst, who need shelter, clothing, freedom from prison.

What will help them—you, me—experience this Presence? That is the burden of this book.

Practices that strengthen awareness

In their worship, Jews may sing, "Holy, holy, holy, the Lord of Hosts. His presence fills all the earth." God fills the world, the universe. God fills time, is present in each moment. Awareness of that Presence does not come easily. It takes practice. There is no magic formula that makes it feel automatic. To experience that Presence we need to develop practices that strengthen that awareness. This book has described various practices that aid in that pursuit. The simplest one, however, and perhaps the hardest one, is to live in—be aware of—each moment. There, in the present, is reality. There also is Reality, God's presence, whether the moment comes amid pleasure or pain, ease or difficulty, joy or sorrow. In each moment, God is. And not just is, but loves. God's presence is a loving presence, whether that love feels cuddly or harsh, warm or indifferent.

People describe what I call an experience of God's presence in various ways and do not limit it to religious followers. Many see it as a universal longing. In his book *A Secular Age*, Charles Taylor writes,

> We all see our lives, and/or the space wherein we live our lives, as having a certain moral/spiritual shape. Somewhere, in some activity or condition, lies a fullness, a richness: that is, in that place (activity or condition), life is fuller, richer, deeper, more worthwhile, more admirable, more what it should be. This is perhaps a place of power: we often experience this as deeply moving, as inspiring. Perhaps this sense of fullness is something we just catch glimpses of from afar off; we have the powerful intuition of what fullness would be, were we to be in that condition, e.g., of peace or wholeness; or able to act on that level, of integrity or generosity or abandonment or self-forgetfulness. But sometimes there will be moments of experienced fullness, of joy and fulfillment, where we feel ourselves there.

Spirituality is about living in that fullness or richness, that wholeness, or what the Bible calls shalom. In our world today, such an experience is usually seen as individual, as fleeting, as primarily emotional or perhaps intellectual.

I argue that Mennonite spirituality (perhaps more the prescriptive than the descriptive notion) extends that experience toward being communal, ongoing and holistic, including the body in all its aspects.

In other words, wholeness is to be an everyday (every moment) affair, ordinary. It is not necessarily special or spectacular—no wow factor—though that may happen, just as suffering and sadness may happen. By living in each moment, in communion with others, in every aspect of our lives—not just the so-called holy activities—we engage God's presence, surrendering ourselves to God with thanks.

Such living is not easy; it requires much practice. Being in relationship with others and giving ourselves to them provides us with much practice. It's usually not the heroic actions but the little things that are most difficult. Being interrupted by someone needing something from us just as we're involved in something we enjoy may be much harder than volunteering to help storm victims or giving a sermon.

Each day gives us opportunities to practice this self-surrender, which I've called Gelassenheit. This is at the heart of Mennonite spirituality. It is also at the heart of biblical faithfulness.

When Mary said, "Let it be with me according to your word" (Luke 1:38b), she was practicing Gelassenheit.

When Jesus prayed in Gethsemane, "Not my will but yours be done" (Luke 22:42b), he was practicing Gelassenheit.

When the disciples asked Jesus who is the greatest in the kingdom of heaven, he put a child among them and said, "Whoever becomes humble like this child is the greatest in the kingdom of heaven" (Matt. 18:1-5).

This is not meant to romanticize children but offers a clue to how to live in the kingdom, in tune with God's rule. Such a childlike stance involves recognizing we are not in charge; God rules. It means working with what we have, playing the hand we're dealt. (And perhaps the key word in that familiar phrase is not "dealt," which implies a kind of fatalism, but "playing," which implies freedom of movement and a carefree joy.)

Children also teach us about living in the present. They play, then come to the table when called, not worried about where the food came from.

Jesus pointed to the birds as examples of such carefree trust. "Don't worry about your life," he said (Matt. 6:25). You only think you're in control. Don't be like "the Gentiles, who strive for all these things" (6:22). They (perhaps the Romans are in hearers' minds) only seem to be in control. Really God is. So strive to live in that reality. "Tomorrow will bring worries of its own," Jesus sums up (6:34). "Today's trouble is enough for today."

I know this can sound pollyanish, unrealistic. You have to make plans for tomorrow. Food doesn't just show up on the table; someone has to buy it and prepare it. Yes, but don't let those concerns rule you. Believe you are in God's hands and act on that truth. As we plan tomorrow's work or meals, we do so in the present moment. And we do so with the knowledge that those plans may have to change.

This nonanxious presence in the present is not something we learn overnight. It takes discipline. One of the elements of Benedictine discipline is called "statio." This is the practice of pausing between activities to become conscious of the moment, of the presence of God. Try it.

• • •

This book has been an exploration of Mennonite spirituality. Both words invite debate as to their meanings. Mennonites love to talk about the former—and this book may serve as the best proof that I am one—but the latter not so much. They let Catholics discuss spirituality.

I've looked at the term *Mennonite* in descriptive and prescriptive ways and asked, What lies at the heart of who we are and who we strive to be? In my thirty-plus years as a Mennonite journalist I've read and written many stories about Mennonites from around the world. I've watched them fight, laugh, pray, sing, work, even play. I've participated in these activities as well, and I've noted qualities that I've liked and disliked.

When I discuss Mennonite practice, patience, peace, politics, play, prayer, perfection, and presence, I'm fully aware these are performed (another P) imperfectly, even messily. But they are there, at the center of their often unarticulated faith. I want to invite them (and anyone else) to that center.

Spirituality, I've noted, is living in (and by) the Spirit. It is not a strategy or tactic, not a rule or lesson but a life. And living, as we all know, is usually mundane, messy and unpredictable.

Living in the present may seem like some new-age practice borrowed from Buddhism, but it describes what Jesus called "eternal life." It fits with what the early Anabaptists called "Gelassenheit." Opening ourselves to what *is* (and that two-letter word names the present), understanding that we cannot control the past or future, that we live under the canopy of God's grace, is a way of imitating our Lord Jesus, whose incarnated life showed us what it's like to live in the harmony of God's triune love.

This living in the present places us in the tension between what is and the shalom God is drawing us (and the universe) toward. Such tension makes this kind of living difficult and often complex. But God's Spirit animates our practice and offers a free-flowing forgiveness that allows us to leave behind our faltering steps and walk on in the moment, which is ever new, ever beautiful.

Bibliography

Alter, Robert (2009) *The Book of Psalms: A Translation with Commentary*. New York: W.W. Norton and Co.

Anonymous (1978). *The Cloud of Unknowing*. New York: Penguin Books.

Anonymous (1978). *The Way of a Pilgrim* and *The Pilgrim Continues His Way*. Garden City, N.Y.: Image Books.

Auden, W. H. (1991). *Collected Poems*. New York: Vintage International.

Augustine (1993). *Confessions*. London: The Folio Society.

Ausburger, David (2006). *Dissident Discipleship: A Spirituality of Self-Surrender, Love of God, and Love of Neighbor*. Grand Rapids, Mich.: Brazos Press.

Barrett, Lois (1987). *The Way God Fights: War and Peace in the Old Testament*. Scottdale, Pa.: Herald Press.

Beckett, Lucy (2006). *In the Light of Christ: Writings in the Western Tradition*. San Francisco: Ignatius Press.

Begbie, Jeremy (2007). *Resounding Truth: Christian Wisdom in the World of Music*. Grand Rapids, Mich.: Baker.

Bloom, Anthony (1971). *God and Man*. Maryknoll, N.Y.: Paulist Press.

Boers, Arthur Paul (2003). *The Rhythm of God's Grace: Uncovering Morning and Evening Hours of Prayer*. Brewster, Mass.: Paraclete Press.

Boers, Arthur Paul, Barbara Nelson Gingerich, Eleanor Kreider, John Rempel, and Mary H. Schertz, ed. (2007). *Take Our Moments and Our Days: An Anabaptist Prayer Book: Ordinary Time*. Scottdale, Pa.: Herald Press.

Bonhoeffer, Dietrich (1954). *Life Together*. New York: Harper & Brothers.

Borg, Marcus (2003). *The Heart of Christianity: Rediscovering a Life of Faith*. San Francisco: Harper.

Brimlow, Robert W. (2006). *What About Hitler? Wrestling with Jesus' Call to Nonviolence in an Evil World*. Grand Rapids, Mich.: Brazos Press.

Brother Lawrence (1958). *The Practice of the Presence of God*. Old Tappan, N.J.: Fleming H. Revell.

Buechner, Frederick (1980). *Godric: A Novel*. New York: Atheneum.

Cahill, Thomas (1999). *Desire of the Everlasting Hills: The World Before and After Jesus*. New York: Doubleday.

Caputo, John D. (2006). *Philosophy and Theology*, Nashville, Tenn.: Abington Press.

——— (2007). *What Would Jesus Deconstruct? The Good News of Postmodernism for the Church*. Grand Rapids, Mich.: BakerAcademic.

Cavanaugh, William T. (2008). *Being Consumed: Economics and Christian Desire*. Grand Rapids, Mich.: Eerdmans.

——— (2002). *Celebrating Common Prayer*. New York: Continuum.

Chilson, Richard W. (2004). *Meditation: Exploring the Great Spiritual Practice*. Notre Dame, Ind.: Sorin Books.

Clapp, Rodney (2000). *Border Crossings: Christian Trespasses on Popular Culture and Public Affairs*. Grand Rapids, Mich.: Brazos Press.

Clemens, Philip K. (2007). *Beyond the Law: Living Sermon on the Mount*. Scottdale, Pa.: Herald Press.

Clément, Olivier (1995). *The Roots of Christian Mysticism*. New York: New City Press.

Confession of Faith in a Mennonite Pespective (1995). Scottdale, Pa.: Herald Press.

Csikszentmihalyi, Michaly (1990). *Flow: The Psychology of Optimal Experience*. New York: Harper & Row.

Dark, David (2005). *The Gospel According to America: A Meditation on a God-blessed, Christ-Haunted Idea*. Louisville, Ky.: Westminster John Knox Press.

De Caussade, Jean-Pierre (1975). *Abandonment to Divine Providence*. Garden City, N.Y.: Image Books.

De Mello, Anthony (1990). *Awareness*. New York: Doubleday.

De Waal, Esther (1997). *The Celtic Way of Prayer: The Recovery of the Religious Imagination*. New York: Doubleday.

De Wit, Hans, Louis Jonker, Marlene Kool and Daniel Schipani, ed. (2004). *Through the Eyes of Another: Intercultural Reading of the Bible*. Elkhart, Ind.: Institute of Mennonite Studies.

Dillard, Annie (1977). *Holy the Firm*. New York: Harper Colophon Books.

——— (1974). *Pilgrim at Tinker Creek*. New York: Bantam Books.

Dostoevsky, Fyodor, trans. Richard Pevear and Larissa Volokhonsky (1990). *The Brothers Karamozov: A Novel*. New York: North Point Press.

Dyck, Cornelius J., ed. (1981). *An Introduction to Mennonite History: A Popular History of the Anabaptists and the Mennonites*. Scottdale, Pa.: Herald Press.

Finger, Reta Halteman (2007). *Of Widows and Meals: Communal Meals in the Book of Acts*. Grand Rapids, Mich.: Eerdmans.

Finley, James (2004). *Christian Meditation: Experiencing the Presence of God*. San Francisco: Harper.

Forest, Jim (2008). *Praying with Icons*. Maryknoll, N.Y.: Orbis Books.

Hahn, Thich Nhat (1987). *Being Peace*. Berkeley, Calif.: Parallax Press.

Hansen, Ron (2001). *A Stay Against Confusion: Essays on Faith and Fiction*. San Francisco: HarperCollins.

Haught, John F. (2008). *God and the New Atheism: A Critical Response to Dawkins, Harris and Hitchens*, Louisvill, Ky.: Westminster John Knox Press.

Hawking, Stephen with Leonard Mlodinow (2005). *A Briefer History of Time*. New York: Bantam.

Houser, Gordon (1995, Feb. 28). "As Often As You Do This." *The Mennonite*.

——— (1996, July 23). "Call Me Mennonite." *The Mennonite*.

——— (2007, Sept. 18). "Embodied Faith." *The Mennonite*.

——— (1990, June 12). "'Mennonite Christian' Is Redundant." *The Mennonite*.

——— (2000, Aug. 15). "Present Tense." *The Mennonite*.

Keating, Thomas (1996). *Invitation to Love: An Introduction to Centering Prayer*. New York: Crossroad.

Kelly, Thomas R. (1941). *A Testament of Devotion*. San Francisco: Harper.

Kern, Kathleen (2008). *In Harm's Way: A History of Christian Peacemaker Teams*. Eugene, Ore.: Wipf and Stock.

Kisly, Lorraine, ed. (2002). *Watch and Pray: Christian Teachings on the Practice of Prayer*. New York: Bell Tower.

Kraybill, Donald B. (1978). *The Upside-Down Kingdom*. Scottdale, Pa.: Herald Press.

Kraybill, Donald B., Steven M. Nolt and David C. Weaver-Zercher (2007). *Amish Grace: How Forgiveness Transcended Tragedy*. San Francisco: Jossey-Bass.

Kropf, Marlene. (2007, Sept. 4). "A Modest Proposal for Communion." *The Mennonite*.

Levy, Sandra M. (2008). *Imagination and the Journey of Faith*. Grand Rapids, Mich.: Eerdmans.

McClendon, James Wm., Jr. (1986). *Systemic Theology: Ethics*. Nashville, Tenn.: Abington Press.

McIntyre, Alasdair (1984). *After Virtue: A Study in Moral Theory*. South Bend, Ind.: University of Notre Dame Press.

Merton, Thomas (1973). *Contemplation in a World of Action*. Garden City, N.Y.: Image Books.

———— (1973). *Contemplative Prayer*. Garden City, N.Y.: Image Books.

———— (1961). *New Seeds of Contemplation*. New York: New Directions.

———— (1960). *The Wisdom of the Desert*. New York: New Directions.

Moore, Sebastian (2008). *The Contagion of Jesus: Doing Theology As If It Mattered*. Maryknoll, N.Y.: Orbis Books.

Myss, Caroline (2007). *Entering the Castle: An Inner Path to God and Your Soul*. New York: Free Press.

Neiman, Susan (2002). *Evil in Modern Thought: An Alternative History of Philosophy*. Princeton , N.J.: Princeton University Press.

Newell, J. Philip (2008). *Christ of the Celts: The Healing of Creation*. San Francisco: Jossey-Bass.

Nouwen, Henri J. M. (1987). *Behold the Beauty of the Lord: Praying with Icons*. Notre Dame, Ind.: Ave Maria Press.

————. (1979). *Clowning in Rome:Reflections on Solitude, Celibacy, Prayer and Contemplation*. Garden City, N.Y.: Image Books.

————. (1981). *The Way of the Heart*. New York: Seabury Press.

O'Collins, Gerald (2008). *Jesus: A Portrait*. Maryknoll, N.Y.: Orbis Books.

Oliver, Mary (2006). *Thirst: Poems*. Boston: Beacon Press.

Paulsell, Stephanie (2002). *Honoring the Body: Meditations on a Christian Practice*. San Francisco: Jossey-Bass.

Peterson, Eugene H. (2007). *Christ Plays in Ten Thousand Places: A Conversation on the Ways That Jesus Is the Way*. Grand Rapids, Mich.: Eerdmans.

———— (2005). *The Jesus Way: A Conversation in Spiritual Theology*. Grand Rapids, Mich.: Eerdmans.

Placher, William C. (2007). *The Triune God: An Essay in Postliberal Theology*. Louisville, Ky.: Westminster John Knox Press.

Picard, Max (2002). *The World of Silence*. Wichita, Kan.: Eighth Day Press.

Polkinghorne, John (2005). *Exploring Reality: The Intertwining of Science and Religion*. New Haven, Conn.: Yale University Press.

Rempel, John D. (1993). *The Lord's Supper in Anabaptism: A Study in the Christology of Balthasar Hubmaier, Pilgram Marpeck and Dirk Philips*. Scottdale, Pa.: Herald Press.

Rohr, Richard (2003). *Everything Belongs: The Gift of Contemplative Prayer*. New York: Crossroad.

——— (1996). *Job and the Mystery of Suffering: Spiritual Reflections*. New York: Crossroad.

——— and Andreas Ebert (2002). *The Enneagram: A Christian Perspective*. New York: Crossroad.

Rolheiser, Ronald (2001). *Against an Infinite Horizon: The Finger of God in Our Everyday Lives*. New York: Crossroad.

——— (1999). *The Holy Longing: The Search for a Christian Spirituality*. New York: Doubleday.

——— 2007, Aug. 17). "Infinite Spirits in a Finite World," (interview). *National Catholic Reporter,*

Ross, Maggie (1987). *The Fountain and the Furnace*. New York: Paulist Press.

Roth, John D. (2005). *Beliefs: Mennonite Faith and Practice*. Scottdale, Pa.: Herald Press.

——— (2006). *Stories: How Mennonites Came to Be*. Scottdale, Pa.: Herald Press.

——— (2009) *Practices: Mennonite Worship and Witness*. Scottdale, Pa.: Herald Press.

Ruth, John L. (2007). *Forgiveness: A Legacy of the West Nickel Mines Amish School*. Scottdale, Pa.: Herald Press.

Sine, Tom (2008). *The New Conspirators: Creating the Future One Mustard Seed at a Time*. Downers Grove, Ill.: InterVarsity Press.

Smith, Allyne, annotator (2006). *The Philokalia: The Eastern Christian Spiritual Texts*. Woodstock, Vt.: SkyLight Paths.

Snodgrass, Klyne R. (2008). *Stories with Intent: A Comprehensive Guide to the Parables of Jesus*. Grand Rapids, Mich.: Eerdmans.

Snyder, Arnold C. (2004). *Following in the Footsteps of Christ: The Anabaptist Tradition.* Maryknoll, N.Y.: Orbis Books.

Solovyov, Vladimir (1996). *The Crisis of Western Philosophy.* Hudson, N.Y.: Lindisfarne Press.

St. John of the Cross (1959). *The Dark Night of the Soul.* Garden City, N.Y.: Image.

St. Teresa of Avila (1960). *The Life of Teresa of Jesus.* Garden City, N.Y.: Image Books.

Steindl-Rast, David (1984). *Gratefulness: The Heart of Prayer: An Approach to Life in Fullness.* New York: Paulist Press.

Stewart, Elizabeth-Anne (1999). *Jesus the Holy Fool.* Kansas City, Mo.: Sheed & Ward.

Swartley, Willard M. (2007). *Covenant of Peace: The Missing Peace to New Testament Theology and Ethics.* Grand Rapids, Mich.: Eerdmans.

Taylor, Charles (2007). *A Secular Age.* Cambridge, Mass.: Belknap Press.

The Rutba House, ed. (2005). *School(s) for Conversion: 12 Marks of a New Monastacism.* Eugene, Ore.: Cascade Books.

Thiessen, Linda (1990, July 24). Letter to the Editor, "A non-Christian Mennonite." *The Mennonite.*

Tickle, Phyllis (2008). *The Great Emergence.* Grand Rapids, Mich.: Baker Books.

Tolle, Eckhart (1999). *The Power of Now.* Novato, Calif.: New World Library.

——— (2003). *Stillness Speaks.* Novato, Calif.: New World Library.

Valantasis, Richard (2005). *Centuries of Holiness: Ancient Spirituality Refracted for a Postmodern Age.* New York: Continuum.

Ware, Timothy (1984). *The Orthodox Church.* New York: Penguin Books.

——— (1979). *The Orthodox Way.* Crestwood, N.Y.: St. Vladimir's Seminary Press.

Webber, Robert (2008). *Ancient-Future Worship: Proclaiming and Enacting God's Narrative.* Grand Rapids, Mich.: Baker.

Wilber, Ken (2000). *A Brief History of Everything.* Boston: Shambhala.

———(2000). *The Eye of Spirit.* Boston: Shambhala.

Williams, Rowan (2007). *Tokens of Trust: An Introduction to Christian Belief.* Louisville, Ky.: Westminster John Knox Press.

Wilson-Hartgrove, Jonathan (2008). *New Monasticism: What It Has to Say to Today's Church.* Grand Rapids, Mich.: Brazos Press.

Wolterstorff, Nicholas (1987). *Lament for a Son*. Grand Rapids, Mich.: Eerdmans.

Woods, Richard J. (2006). *Christian Spirituality: God's Presence Through the Ages*. Maryknoll, N.Y.: Orbis Books.

Yoder, John Howard (1971) *Nevertheless: Varieties of Religious Pacifism*. Scottdale, Pa.: Herald Press.

———— (1972). *The Politics of Jesus*. Grand Rapids, Mich.: Eerdmans.

———— (1983). *What Would You Do? A Serious Answer to a Standard Question*. Scottdale, Pa.: Herald Press.

Yoder, Perry B. (1987). *Shalom: The Bible's Word for Salvation, Justice, and Peace*, Newton, Kan.: Faith and Life Press.

York, Tripp (2008). *The Purple Crown*. Scottdale, Pa.: Herald Press.

Young, Frances M. (2007). *Brokenness and Blessing: Towards a Biblical Spirituality*. Grand Rapids, Mich.: BakerAcademic.

The Author

Gordon Houser is a long-time Mennonite journalist and church member who came to the Mennonite faith as a young adult. He is the author of *Relatively Speaking: Strengthening Families Ties* and contributed to *Wrestling with God: Devotions for Men*. Born in 1953 in Emporia, Kansas, the youngest of seven, he graduated from Wichita (Kan.) State University in 1976 with a B.A. in linguistics. After college he joined New Creation Fellowship, an intentional Christian community and a Mennonite congregation in Newton, Kansas.

In 1978 Houser began working for *The Mennonite*, the periodical of the General Conference Mennonite Church, as editorial assistant. He became assistant editor in 1984 and editor in 1992. In 1998, that magazine merged with *Gospel Herald*, the periodical of the Mennonite Church, and became *The Mennonite*, which Houser now serves as associate editor. He continues to be active in New Creation Fellowship Church, which is no longer an intentional community but remains a Mennonite congregation. Houser is married to Jeanne, and they have two children, both married.

NOV – – 2012 L V

BW
April 6

CPSIA information can be obtained at www.ICGtesting.com
Printed in the USA
LVOW102127121011

250228LV00003B/15/P

9 781931 038904